Cass Gilbert Abroad

Maison Pimont, Rouen

Library of Congress

CASS GILBERT ABROAD
The Young Architect's European Tour

Paul Clifford Larson

To Linda & Jack

July 28, 2011

AFTON HISTORICAL SOCIETY PRESS
AFTON, MINNESOTA

Front–cover illustration: Street scene in Chartres. Library of Congress

Back–cover illustration: Cathedral apse at twilight, Nevers, France. Library of Congress

Edited by Michele Hodgson
Pre Press and Printing by Pettit Network Inc Afton, MN

Printed in China

Library of Congress Cataloging-in-Publication Data

Larson, Paul Clifford.
  Cass Gilbert abroad: the young architect's European
tour / Paul Clifford Larson. 1st ed.
      p. cm.
Includes bibliographical note.
  ISBN 1-890434-51-5 (alk. paper)
  1. Gilbert, Cass, 1859–1934—Correspondence. 2. Architects—United
States—Correspondence. 3. Gilbert, Cass, 1859–1934—Notebooks,
sketchbooks, etc. 4. Gilbert, Cass, 1859–1934—Journeys—Europe.
I. Title.
  NA737.G5 A3 2002
  720'.92—dc21
                                    2002005035

The Afton Historical Society Press publishes exceptional books on regional subjects.

W. Duncan MacMillan
President

Patricia Condon Johnston
Publisher

Afton Historical Society Press
P.O. Box 100, Afton, MN 55001
800-436-8443
aftonpress@aftonpress.com
www.aftonpress.com

I am learning to live, and to see beauty in everything.
Cass Gilbert, St. Antheme, France, 1880

Norman doorway, church at Serquigny.

Contents

Cass Gilbert in 1880

Minnesota Historical Society

PREFACE

The last decades of the twentieth century brought a heightened awareness of how much beauty resides in the architecture despised by early modernists. Louis H. Sullivan and Frank Lloyd Wright will always be icons of American architecture, but they now stand in a light shared by a host of their contemporaries with unabashed sympathies for the ancient European past. Among the leaders of this latter group, and as immersed in European traditions as any architect could be, was Cass Gilbert.

Gilbert's illustrious architectural career dawned in his twentieth year, not with an American building but with a sheaf of European sketches. In 1880 he crossed the Atlantic with high hopes but only the vaguest prospect of work, either abroad or on his return. Armed with pencil, pen, and watercolor brushes, he visually raided the cities and countrysides of England, Italy, and France for their architectural wonders, their scenery, and anything else that served his fascination with the monumental and the picturesque. He returned home bitterly disappointed at not finding a position in England; but the spoils he brought back—a matchless portfolio of studies and sketches—earned him entrée into one of the foremost architectural offices in the country, gave him his first published work, and served as the foundation for a long and fruitful career.

Among all of Gilbert's European pilgrimages—and there were a dozen more—this first tour would always occupy a special place. It informed and nurtured an architectural vision that never ceased searching for a conciliation between the pictorial and the monumental, the Gothic and the classical. It also gave rise to the first moments of his enduring legacy as an artist cum architect.

The achievements of Gilbert's maturity—in particular, the Woolworth Building in New York City and the U.S. Supreme Court Building in Washington, D.C.— now bask under a steady beam of scholarship. It is only fitting that these earliest glimmerings of his talent, strong enough even then to win acclaim among his peers in New York and Paris, should at last be brought into the light.

We are fortunate to have at our fingertips a trove of materials on Gilbert's first grand tour, most of it created by the architect himself and retained for many years by his heirs. His evocative letters from Europe now reside at the Minnesota Historical Society and in the Manuscripts Division of the Library of Congress. His cache of drawings and sketches has been split into separate collections at the Prints and Photographs Division of the Library of Congress, the National Museum of American Art of the Smithsonian Institution, and the Department of Prints, Photographs, and Architectural Collections of the New-York Historical Society. I am grateful to the energetic staffs of each of these superb resource centers for ensuring my access to all of the relevant materials. The Avery Architectural and Fine Arts Library of Columbia University holds several photo albums assembled by Gilbert and his namesake son, as well as an assortment of memorabilia that Gilbert's mentor at MIT, William Robert Ware, brought with him when setting up the architecture department at Columbia University. Both collections have materials relating to Gilbert's student years, and I am grateful to Lou Di Gennaro of the manuscripts staff for making them accessible to me.

My indebtedness to Patricia Johnston and the Afton Press for their support and encouragement continues. A project focusing on Cass Gilbert's early career in Minnesota has been a work in progress for several years. But the press wisely decided to publish first this even earlier aspect of Gilbert's creative accomplishments, as a sort of initial installment of the thesis that his genius flowered long before his move to New York gave it the opportunity to make its mark on the urban American landscape.

Gilbert's drawing of his own accomplishments placed among world monuments, 1915
Library of Congress

INTRODUCTION

I n January 1880 Cass Gilbert embarked on a European tour that would set the stage for a remarkable career in architecture. Barely past his twentieth birthday, the Zanesville, Ohio, native studied, sketched, and marveled at ancient buildings and landscapes with the wistful conviction that he would one day stand shoulder to shoulder with their creators. In another ten years he would begin to sense, with the completion of a St. Paul, Minnesota, building inspired by Florentine palaces, that he was at the portal of this world, seeking entry not as an onlooker but as a creative participant.

Flush with the triumph of his design for the Minnesota State Capitol, Gilbert would return to Europe a second time in 1897, confident at last of being on speaking terms—figuratively, at least—with the Italian Renaissance masters. Like English Renaissance master Inigo Jones almost three hundred years earlier, Gilbert sought out their work for solutions to problems specific to projects anticipated or already under way.

Gilbert deliberately chose his first tour abroad over finishing his formal training in architecture at the Massachusetts Institute of Technology. The explosive expansion of his practice at the turn of the century was fueled by the carefully recorded discoveries of those first two tours, and for the remainder of his life he looked to his transcontinental excursions as his real school. A succession of eclectic, European-saturated monuments poured from his New York office: the Fifth Street Building, the U.S. Customs House, the Broadway Chambers Building, and the pioneering Woolworth skyscraper, to name those arising in Lower Manhattan alone. Even when his success was ensured, Gilbert would return again and again to that same self-schooling of European travel and sketching for guidance and inspiration. The full-blown neoclassical style of his last project, the U.S. Supreme Court Building, is final testament to that allegiance.

In undertaking his first European tour, Gilbert was well aware of a larger picture as well. Traveling abroad was widely regarded as the proper way to achieve social standing and along the way polish off the process of becoming a gentleman. This was a centuries-old tradition in the English-speaking world. As Sidney Lee remarks, "The value of foreign travel as a means of education was never better understood, in spite of rudimentary means of locomotion, than by the upper classes of Elizabethan England."[1] By focusing on architecture, Gilbert's travels also echo those of the first great English neoclassicist, Inigo Jones (1573–1652).

Firsthand exposure to new architectural currents attracted the young architect of late Victorian America to the Continent as surely as it had his forebear in Renaissance England. Italy and France during the sixteenth century were rediscovering and redefining the architectural glories of ancient Greece and Rome, while England under Elizabeth clung stubbornly to Gothicism. Three hundred years later American architecture for the most part proceeded with no more cognizance than Tudor England of the resurgent tide of neoclassicism on the Continent. Though not stagnating in Gothicism strictly defined, American architecture after the Civil War was caught up in a flurry of "picturesque" styles that Gilbert's early contemporaries sometimes grouped under the rubric "Gothic." All were loosely based on European precedent, but they were already deemed old-fashioned by the American avant-garde, and their unbridled eclecticism ignored (or defied) the current French and German impetus toward a convergent set of academically grounded aesthetic ideals.

Access to a specialized formal education also placed many of Gilbert's peers, and Jones's later contemporaries, on Continental soil, though Gilbert and Jones themselves were denied that opportunity. At the time Jones first went to Italy, Oxford and Cambridge universities, though established three and four centuries earlier, still offered no architectural curriculum. The term "architect" had barely crept into the English language. Those wishing to study building as an art rather than an artifact of construction thus had to look to schools in Germany and France. Analogously, no college or university in America could boast a course of study in architecture in 1880, save a technical school in Boston. And the curriculum of that school—the Massachusetts Institute of Technology—consciously and proudly claimed the École des Beaux-Arts in Paris as its parent. Every American department or school of architecture established before World War I would follow suit.

During his stays in Paris in 1880, Gilbert frequently expressed a longing to be engaged as a student at the École des Beaux-Arts. He lacked the money to do so and, because of his early exit from MIT, probably lacked the academic qualifications as well. But his precocious skills at rendering and analyzing buildings were immediately recognized by the community of students and artists in the Latin Quarter, and he saw himself as their peer. The Americans among them knew they were studying at the world's finest training ground for architects, with the models for their studies all about them—and thousands of miles removed from any place where they were likely to practice their profession.

This last point was critical. Travel abroad offered the fledgling architect an opportunity to overleap the limitations of his native built environment. Jones's trips to Italy were driven by a conviction that its monuments, both ancient and recent, had the most to teach a modern architect. The contemporary culture of Italy was, in Edward Chaney's words, "as impressive as its past and in many respects still outshone their own." Andrea Palladio (1508–1580) was a case in point, and Jones invested a good deal of his time studying Palladio's numerous villas in and around Venice.[2]

For the nineteenth-century American the situation was even more acute; every nation in Europe boasted an artistic and architectural heritage hundreds and sometimes thousands of years richer than his own. Moreover, England, France, and Germany swarmed with architects whose expertise in ancient-building style and practice could scarcely be matched by those who did not grow up among the monuments expected to serve as models for their own practice. Like many of his compatriots abroad, Gilbert saw European travel as a way of invigorating American art and architecture by connecting them in as informed a way as possible to their European roots.

Last, the European tour promised young artists and architects an advance in professional standing that could hardly be earned any other way. Jones was a painter without social standing until he went to Florence to study painting and theater at the Medici court around 1600. Shortly afterward, he received his first royal commission: to provide costumes and settings for a masque. A growing interest in architecture, perhaps stimulated by this early trip, culminated in a tour of northern Italy in 1613–1614, this time under the patronage of art collector and powerful

Catholic nobleman Thomas Howard, Lord Arundel. Though ostensibly there to advance Lord Arundel's interests, Jones studied and sketched Roman ruins as well as buildings by Palladio. On his return, he was appointed surveyor of the king's works, largely an honorary post before Jones parlayed it into a lofty architectural position from which he could oversee all buildings erected under the patronage of the crown—and play a direct role in the design of many of them.[3]

Like his famed English predecessor, Gilbert anticipated a dramatic outcome for his first trip abroad. In the 1850s, Richard Morris Hunt had led the way for American architects by following a distinguished tenure as a student at the École des Beaux-Arts with two years of travel through Europe, Asia Minor, and the Near East. Hunt arrived in New York, in the words of Henry van Brunt, "accredited as an ambassador of art from the abounding wealth of the old world to the infinite possibilities of the new." Gilbert's vision, though humbler in scope, was equally optimistic. Writing to Clarence Johnston, his closest friend and architectural confidant, six months before he embarked, Gilbert already anticipated a return "home to America, fitted for a life of usefulness and with a sound foundation for ambition, with a reasonable hope of success in life and a name in my profession."[4]

The centuries intervening between Inigo Jones's second tour of Italy and Gilbert's first tour of Europe brought many changes to the way English-speaking gentlemen regarded the Continental tour. By the mid-eighteenth century, Englishmen were aware of being from the most powerful nation in the Western world, with a rising artistic and architectural presence that no longer looked for endorsement from current work abroad. Robert Adam's capture on paper of the exquisite detailing of Pompeiian ornament was as much a coup for English pride as Lord Elgin's wresting of marble figures from the Acropolis.

An Italian imperative remained supreme, but it had narrowed to past accomplishments wrought on Italy's soil. Renaissance achievements melded with those of ancient Rome, Naples, and Pompeii, creating a sort of walking museum for the tourist. In addition, the "picturesque" had emerged as an important aesthetic category, and the setting of the walking museum in a landscape begging for pictorialization became as important a component of its appreciation as the character of the monuments themselves.

Out of this mix of aesthetic ideals, national pride, and professional aspirations arose the artist's grand tour of continental Europe as Gilbert experienced it. For the mid-nineteenth-century architect abroad, the Continent offered both the famed monuments of the past and an endless sequence of architectural environments capable of inspiring genuinely new work.

During the latter half of the nineteenth century, fashionable tours for artists and architects followed closely parallel lines. Each included an itinerary of renowned monuments, historic sites, and museums and focused on France and Italy, with a nod to England, often engendered more by the convenience of a shared language than by any particular regard for its artistic products. Among those particularly attuned to whatever enhancement in their social standing the journey might provide, the ease of social interaction in England was actually a detriment, for it compromised the "foreign" element deemed crucial to the experience.

For American architects of Gilbert's generation, England was a special case, as they tended to view the European past through the eyes of English scholar-architects. Gilbert was no exception. "There are architects in London now," he wrote Johnston, "such as we may never see grouped in another generation of men. Street, Liddon, Waterhouse, Norman Shaw, [and] Burges are names which will belong as well to posterity as to the present age."[5] England was, therefore, the natural point of departure, as well as the first place Gilbert looked for employment at journey's end. London's architecture was another matter, with Christopher Wren's work receiving Gilbert's special censure. Its severity offended him in his youth, just as its simplicity would inspire him in his maturity.

Italy was the first country Gilbert toured extensively; but he whirled from one heavily trod center to another, from Milan to Florence to Venice to Rome, spending more time soaking in the historical ambience, wandering among ruins, and inhabiting museums than sketching architectural monuments. He was plainly overpowered by the wealth of architecture and artifacts laid out before him. But Gilbert also still had too much of the picturesque in him to linger long before buildings without towers, chimneys, and dormers. His few Italian watercolor sketches were largely of ruins and sailboats.

The outstanding exception was an interior of San Marco, which he time and again remarked on for its brilliant color scheme, with little cognizance as yet (if his letters are any measure) of its spatial character. Domed or colonnaded buildings, like Wren's churches, were not the magnet they would become in future tours.

This first taste of Europe reached its climax on French soil. Two areas vied for Gilbert's special attention: the Valley of the Loire and the cathedral towns of Normandy. Richard Morris Hunt had already put the chateaux along the Loire into American dress, and Gilbert's mentor at MIT, William Robert Ware, was particularly fond of the French Renaissance manner they embodied. Normandy, on the other hand, was famed for its Gothic churches, regarded by Gilbert—and many others before and since—as the finest expressions of the style. Though his youthful personal leanings favored Gothicism, he saw the two styles as equally monumental, noble, and picturesque—all favorite adjectives.

Among all of Gilbert's European pilgrimages, the first would remain paramount. It inspired an architectural vision that would never cease reflecting and recasting the glories of the European past. Young Gilbert took advantage of every opportunity to record—via sketches, photographs, and written descriptions—multiple levels of his visual experiences, from overall impressions to the finest level of detail. His literary and artistic gifts sprang to life in a way that neither the rigors of study at MIT nor the boredom of the jobs undertaken to finance his education and travels had permitted.

Highly charged descriptions of landscapes, site plans, and architectural monuments filled forty- and fifty-page letters to his mother, Elizabeth Gilbert, and to his closest friend, Clarence Johnston. They reveal an astonishing sense of self-awareness for so young a man. Gilbert himself was amused at how curious a picture he must have cut on the road: bespectacled (with colored glasses, no less) and dressed in leggings, a loose jacket, and a safari hat, carrying an overstuffed satchel over his shoulder. This was thirty years before the Boy Scouts would make such garb an icon of the soul-filled adventurer.

Gilbert never let his obvious youth and apparent eccentricity stand in his way, however. Badgered by a village mayor in Auvergne, he insisted on his right to do what he was doing undisturbed, avoided arrest by faking a passport, and stalked out of town before the local priest (who could read English) showed up. He mixed freely with artists of international repute in several cities along the way, maintaining a worshipful attitude, particularly for those whose studios were filled with the accoutrements of success, but proudly taking in their mixture of praise and criticism for the products of his ceaseless sketching.

Beyond their sparkling descriptions of his adventures, artistic and otherwise, Gilbert's letters testify to a broader aspect of his European experience. The letters are eloquent witness to his coming of age. He was acutely aware of the approach of his twenty-first birthday in November 1880, and with it a cessation of both the allowance and the financial dependence on his mother that allowed him to postpone the task of making a living. Rather than viewing his travels as a lark, he looked constantly for ways to promote his artistic growth and pave the way for a professional career.

Many sides of Gilbert's maturation came unsought and unexpected. His youthful ideas about people of different backgrounds from his own, for example, were put instantly to the test. He arrived in Europe with prejudices typical of many Americans of his day: the French were dishonest, Italians were dirty, Catholics were superstitious and their priests self-serving, to name the most conspicuous in his letters. But in his unstinting (and sometimes astonished) praise of clean villages, fair-minded innkeepers, and an intelligent peasantry wherever he encountered them, and his bitter renunciation of their opposite, the division between honest and dishonest, orderly and disorderly, greedy and generous, began to lose its ethnic and sectarian overtones. He railed against French officialdom, continued to growl at Catholic "myths," and refused to share a hotel bed with a person of lower social standing, but the many acts of kindness and generosity he experienced undermined his sense of righteous separation from those with whom he differed.

In all these matters, Gilbert's European wanderings fulfilled the lofty aims articulated by the English gentry of "that noble and ancient custom of traveling, a custom so visibly tending to enrich the mind with knowledge, to rectify the judgment, to remove the prejudices of education, to compose the outward manners, and in a word to form the complete gentleman."[6]

Gilbert's correspondence home took three distinctive forms. The briefest and most frequent form was the postcard, which he at one point pledged to write to his mother in St. Paul on a daily basis. Except when lodged for a long period in a single place—London, Paris, or Rome—he religiously adhered to that regimen. Consisting mostly of health and weather reports, they contain little of interest beyond helping us to track his movements from city to city.

Along the way Gilbert also wrote letters "To Ma" numbering anywhere from four to fifty-six pages. These he mailed only when he felt the thoughts he had set out to express had received their full expression. On several occasions, that meant carrying the letter from city to city, adding to it as he found time. Gilbert would have quailed at these letters being published in the form in which they were written, for he was well aware that the rush of his thoughts and his haste to use available time and light led to lapses in spelling and organization. But their uncorrected frenzy was a perfect medium for the impassioned descriptions and judgments with which they are suffused.

The third kind of correspondence consisted of letters to Clarence Johnston, who was then apprenticing as an architect in St. Paul. Appearing to have been written in one sitting, whatever their length, they distilled from Gilbert's travels all those experiences and reflections he believed most relevant to a fellow architect-in-the-making. The letters shifted between detailed building descriptions and minute advice for Johnston's own anticipated trip abroad. Curiously, the many site plans sketched in Gilbert's correspondence all occurred in his letters to his mother. At this early stage in his development, he was more interested in the plan as an instrument for communicating his experience than he was in the character of the plan in itself.

However eloquent and insightful Gilbert's letters might have been, it is his portfolio of sketches that constitutes the real achievement of his first venture abroad. Like his correspondence, his sketches took a variety of forms and fulfilled a variety of objectives. Most arresting among them to a modern eye is the portfolio of brilliant watercolor sketches. His architectural renderings had received special notice during the second term of his year at MIT, but those tightly conceived essays in line and tone gave little hint of what would flow from his

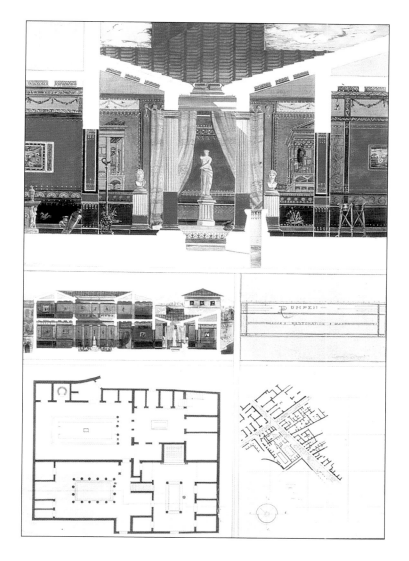

Gilbert's MIT presentation of a restoration at Pompeii
Avery Architectural and Fine Arts Library, Columbia University

brush in Italy and France. Every subject is washed in sunlight and imbued with colors expressive of Gilbert's love of broad and saturated palettes. He everywhere captured massive forms and contours, but touched them with an array of tonalities that made a wall of stone seem picturesque.

From a strictly professional standpoint, the drawings Gilbert most prized were his pen-and-ink renderings. These were the drawings he labored over in his hotel in the evening, straining his already weak eyes to improve upon images first laid down in haste or under unfavorable conditions. They were to be his credentials in America, his means of establishing credibility and reputation in lieu of a completed course of architectural studies. Their acceptance by his peers would, in his view, vindicate both the experience and the skills embodied in them, allowing his career to begin on the same plane as if he bore a diploma from MIT or the École des Beaux-Arts.

Gilbert's immediate future appeared to bear out his hopes. Within days of his return to America, he showed his portfolio to Stanford White of the recently established firm of McKim Mead and White in New York City. By Gilbert's recollection, White "seized one of my European sketches (literally grabbed it) and ran into the next room to show it to Mead with words of praise far beyond its merits." Gilbert had secured his first architectural position. His many mailings of carefully inked sketches to the prestigious *American Architect,* a process initiated while he was still abroad, also began to bear fruit. Five months after his return, two of his European renderings appeared in a single issue, to be followed by a third almost a year later.[7]

For all of the professional hopes Gilbert pinned on his European sketches, his chief motive for devoting so much of his time to drawing remained self-education. For that purpose, pencil was the best tool, permitting greater speed and a higher level of detail than the showier watercolor or painstaking pen-and-ink renderings. Some of his graphite sketches were laid out on individual sheets of folio-sized paper, but most of his pencil drawings went into one of two bound sketchbooks on sheets approximating the size of ordinary writing paper. His folio of drawings, in all media, was shipped in small packets to Paris, London, or Boston as it accumulated, but the sketchbook was forever slung at his side as he walked or rode, a continuous visual journal of his discoveries whatever the weather, however brief the exposure. Some of the pencil sketches were fully rendered, perhaps with a thought to conversion to pen and ink at some future date; others were hastily scrawled with no purpose other than recording a form or detail for future reference.

Among his most charming drawings, rendered in either pen or pencil or both, are miniature studies imbedded in his letters home. All record from memory a particularly vivid impression of the day just past. Though generally lacking the artistry of the larger sketches, they are included here as an integral component of his visual record of this first grand tour.

The sheer volume of Gilbert's sketches and correspondence from his 1880 European venture has necessitated some editing. Nearly all of his folio sketches have been retained, but many pages of the sketchbooks, although of scholarly interest, are either too smudged, too faintly drawn upon, or too jumbled to do them justice in publication.

Similarly, the length and occasional prolixity of his letters has required some abridgment to maintain a focus on the tour itself. Passages of Gilbert's letters describing his experiences or expressing the broad range of his perceptions, moods, and personal and intellectual concerns have, for the most part, been quoted verbatim. But the lengthy assessments of his health and the local weather (which Gilbert took pains to report in detail as a dutiful son) have been omitted, as have his many digressions into family matters.

Gilbert's first European experience had a seismic dimension, often jolting his ambition beyond his reach and inflaming his imagination beyond his capability of bringing it to order. As a profound perfectionist, he undoubtedly would have felt some embarrassment to see these youthful and, in many cases, hasty efforts brought before the public without his having an opportunity to cull and to correct. Even the sketch that won over Stanford White he later regarded as a "poor feeble thing."

Yet the overall quality of Gilbert's literary and visual journaling is astonishingly high. For the sake of clarity and consistency, his occasional lapses in spelling and punctuation have been corrected. But eccentricities in diction and logical order remain as a transparent expression of the quintessential moments of his European venture, when nothing existed but a sketch pad, a glorious architectural monument, and dreams of the soaring career to come.

---

[1] Sidney Lee, *Great Englishmen of the Sixteenth Century*, cited by William Edward Mead, *The Grand Tour in the Eighteenth Century* (Boston and New York: Houghton Mifflin Company, 1914), 1.

[2] Edward Chaney, *The Evolution of the Grand Tour: Anglo-Italian Cultural Relations Since the Renaissance* (London: Frank Crass, 1998), xi.

[3] According to Edward Chaney, Inigo Jones went to Italy with the express purpose of learning to understand classical building. "Inigo Jones in Naples," *The Evolution of the Grand Tour*, 168–202. For a comprehensive treatment of Lord Arundel's career and influence, see David Howarth, *Lord Arundel and His Circle* (New Haven, Conn.: Yale University Press, 1986).

[4] Henry van Brunt quote cited by Ormonde de Kay Jr. in *Three Centuries of Notable American Architects*, ed. by Joseph J. Thorndyke Jr. (American Heritage Publishing Co.: New York, 1981), 95–96; letter to Clarence Johnston, June 22, 1879.

[5] Letter to Clarence Johnston, June 22, 1879.

[6] Lord Nugent, *The Grand Tour; Or, A Journey through the Netherlands, Germany, Italy and France* (London: 1756), cited by William Edward Mead in *The Grand Tour in the Eighteenth Century* (Boston and New York: Houghton Mifflin Company, 1914), 4.

[7] Letter of reminiscences addressed to "Mr. Moore," Sept. 7, 1927; *American Architect and Building News*, vol. 11, n. 268 (Feb. 12, 1881). A third drawing, probably submitted at the same time, was published in *AABN*, vol. 12, n. 317 (Jan. 21, 1882).

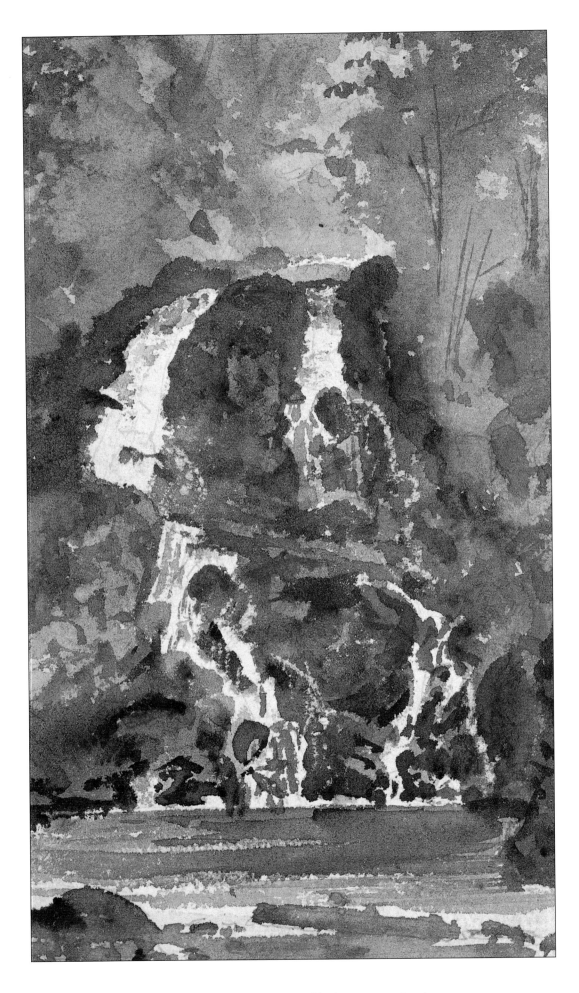

Near Garrisons on the Hudson, New York

Paving the Way

Halfway through the spring term of his 1878–1879 year at the Massachusetts Institute of Technology, Cass Gilbert began to lay plans for an extended European venture. By the beginning of the summer, at work for the U.S. Coast and Geodetic Survey in New York, he was secure enough in his intentions to begin sharing them with his closest friend and architectural ally, Clarence Johnston. Their correspondence reveals much of the thought processes that underlay the grand tour ahead.

From the outset, Gilbert's plans welded pragmatic considerations to his expanding vision of what such a tour could mean to his personal development and his professional career. His mulling over practical matters was suffused with anxieties, many of them fed by a very real financial concern. A stipend of $25 per month from his father's estate had paid for his room and board while in Boston, and he assumed—wrongly, as it turned out—that it would get him by in Europe, so long as he was able to raise the money for transatlantic passage and for inland transportation once he arrived. But that allowance terminated on November 24, 1880, his twenty-first birthday. So if his trip were to embrace even the countries on his short list (England, France, and Italy) it had to be initiated—so he wrote—by the end of 1879.

Had Gilbert envisioned a conventional, high-society-driven grand tour of European monuments, eleven months would have been more than ample time. But he saw it as an all-embracing educational experience, an opportunity to replace the tedium of a three-year course of study at MIT and the mounting tension of student competitions with an equivalent amount of time wandering and sketching on his own. It would not be a frivolous exercise, for he would be studying and recording firsthand the architectural styles and exemplars at the heart of the MIT curriculum. This would be possible only if he stayed on into 1881, past the expiration of his stipend, and that in turn would require finding work abroad.

Gilbert was well aware that talent alone would not open the door to the world he was so impatient to enter. Drawing on a host of connections, from his family's New England ties and his Ohio relatives to Professor William Robert Ware at MIT and a scattering of established architects he had met in Boston, he used every means at his disposal to find a place in a London architectural office. Ruminations over these plans filled his correspondence with Johnston before his trip, just as sorrowings over their defeat set the tone of his final letters home from London.

To Clarence Johnston, June 22, 1879 **Tisbury, Mass.**

I am going to England next fall if my fortunes prosper during the summer as they have in past times. You are going with me. Am I mad? I can almost hear you say as you read this. No, I am perfectly sane and "in reasonable health," and have but one obstacle to combat. My plan briefly, and my first inception of it, roughly skipped over, is this: Last April in writing to Mother . . . I fell to thinking, dreaming of home, of friends, of future prospects, of past experiences, of present difficulties, of ambition, of travel, and of success. . . . My thoughts would wander off to England and its old cathedrals, and almost in a flash came an idea which no sooner came than it was grasped: Living costs no more in England than in America and in Boston. London is the place to live in, if I am in England. Already I am 2,000 miles from home— what difference a few more thousand?

My living is paid by the estate in Boston; it would be in London just the same. . . . Well, this summer I will save about $125.00 out of my work and be clear of debt. This $125.00, with that I would borrow [by previous arrangement with his mother], gives me a capital of $250.00 clear. $75.00 of this will pay my passage clear to London and get me settled there in quiet lodgings (I know my data are right); the remaining $175.00 could lie in bank. Or even suppose I spend $25.00 of it for sundries; I have $150.00 left. This settles the financial question now for the then part, the most important of all.

I go to Europe to study architecture; I go to London because I can't speak French as a principal reason, because London architects impress me from my standpoint as being the most favorable for my purpose, and because from London I can go to Paris; from Paris never could I go to London. There are architects in London now such as we may never see grouped in another generation of men. Street, Liddon, Waterhouse, Norman Shaw, [and] Burges are names which will belong as well to posterity as to the present age, and [they] still live the traditions which Sir Gilbert Scott lived in, and still his work is standard. In London, men who studied with him, worked with him, and were his friends might be known and studied with profit.

My idea is to enter the office of one of these men as a student, giving my time, my labor, and my scanty merit for their instruction and friendship, taking my Saturday afternoons for sketching, my mornings for lectures at the South Kensington and the Art Schools of the city. Canterbury Cathedral is in easy walk of London, Westminster Abbey is on my way to the office. St. Paul's is on my way home to dinner, Windsor Castle but a Sunday afternoon's walk, and the Law Courts but an easy stroll after tea. All England is accessible in a two days' holiday, and I have at hand some of the finest architecture of Christendom.

I could enter the office in November next. I could stay studying and working and trying to get a knowledge of French until the first of June, putting in a full winter's work and gathering loads of information. The 1st of June 1880 I would leave the office and, with my $150.00, my pluck and sketch-book, and my scanty French, go to Paris and to all of France; walking, riding, and wiggling through France, into Italy, into Rome, up to Venice, over to Athens, back to London, and again enter the office in the fall of 1880.

Another year in London as the first was spent, or if I did not want London, Paris is near at hand; and in June 1881 I start back to the charms of Paris, up to Holland, Belgium, and the German States into Austria, up to Russia, back [to] England & Scotland . . . then home to America, fitted for a life of usefulness and with a sound foundation for ambition, with a reasonable hope of success in life and a name in my profession.

This, then, is my project; you have it all. It is feasible, practicable; nothing rests on surmise, nothing on uncertainty, which will not be perfectly clear before I undertake what promises to be so important an event in my life. Come with me, Clarence; share in my purposes and plans. Mother endorses me; Mr. Whiting tells me I am sure of success and will be extremely foolish not to follow my plan. <u>Mr. Ware has promised me all possible help,</u> is warmly enlisted in my cause, <u>is now corresponding with Englishmen</u> in my behalf, has forwarded a letter of mine to a friend of his in London who is to aid me in getting the coveted place in the office of either Street, Waterhouse, Burges, Shaw, or Liddon. He invited me to the meeting of the "A.I.A." [American Institute of Architects] and introduced me to Sturgis of the Society of Boston Architects, and Sturgis (a most courteous gentleman) has promised me letters of introduction to Waterhouse personally. He himself once worked in Waterhouse's office. George T. Tilden has promised me letters to the "Atelier Vandiemer" in Paris and to the "École des Beaux-Artes." Mr. Whiting has promised to get me letters from Prof. Mitchell, Prof. Pierce of Harvard, Mr. Hilgard of the U.S. Coast Survey (Assist. Superintendent), and several others of no less

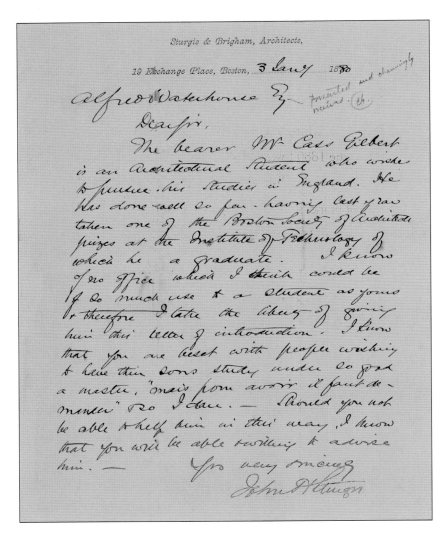

John Sturgis's letter of introduction for Gilbert to Alfred Waterhouse
Library of Congress

importance. . . . Such is a friend at court and such are the rewards of my father's labors; he made friends that I might enjoy their friendship. Is it not glorious that at my age I have opportunities of such magnitude? What puzzles me most is, what is there in me to draw forth such expressions of kindness and regard as I have received of late? True, I have been successful, but is success the virtue which makes one the object [of] commendation or is it merit? It should be merit, if the world were just. Merit I have not, unless ambition be merit and selfishness a virtue. . . .

To Clarence Johnston, July 5, 1879   **West Tisbury, Mass.**

In talking with Mr. Tilden, he says that he corresponded with papers at home when he went abroad and that he has not the slightest doubt but we both could help pay our expenses in that way if necessary. It is my firm intention to correspond with some paper before many months have gone by, [even] if I have to do it for nothing. I am living in a world where opinions make the man, and I am going to learn to express an opinion when I get one. . . .

I shall not probably leave America until the 15th of Nov., if that early.

I should prefer that we should be in separate offices in London if possible, for financial reasons if nothing else. You see, I will have to get a salary my 2nd year or I am busted; and that I could never do with you to compete with.

To Clarence Johnston, July 21, 1879   **Garrisons on the Hudson**

I am worked to death here and have not had time for even the luxury of correspondence. . . . I am disposed to put off my date of departure later even than I first mentioned. The money I save this summer is a great factor in my success, and the more I make, the better chance I'll have in Europe.

What you say of Norman Shaw strikes a kindred note in me. . . . I have pronounced for Street first, Waterhouse second, Shaw third, and Burges fourth as my choice; and I have held to Street as my man.

I am disgusted with myself; I find myself considering a man's academical training rather than his work, and my mind is cramped down to the narrow limits of style, correctness, usage, and tradition rather than beauty, truth, and love of art. I wish, Clarence, I could return to the time when, even though ignorantly, I had the common sense and honesty to declare for what I thought <u>right</u> rather than what I thought <u>proper.</u> The time will come someday when I will not only use my own Ins. training, but my brains also. I am afraid now the latter factor is out of the calculations and I feel and think like my abomination, "a classical architect." Which of Ruskin's works shall I read as an antidote?

To Clarence Johnston, Aug. 3   **Garrisons**

The office I wish to get into is that of George E. Street; his brilliant genius, widespread fame and scholarly manner, his endeavor after pure Gothic, and his surprising exactness of detail in all his office work have an attraction for me that even the romantic spell of Norman Shaw can not overcome. . . .

I am sick of this work here and I do not consider my pay, $45.00 a month, and the official position of "Ass't-Aid U.S. Coast & Geodetic Survey" as any compensation for the work I do. . . . So I am awfully out of the world here and can't get used to it yet.

To Clarence Johnston, Aug. 26, 1879   **Garrisons**

Your acknowledgement of your inability to undertake the trip to Europe with me has caused me to reflect much upon the dispensations of Providence, who, having some good end always in view for us, yet constantly in his wisdom, sees fit to cross our most pure and heartfelt wishes. . . .

As the fall draws on, I am more uncertain as to when I shall leave. . . .

Your advice about entering the office of some young man in London in preference to entering no office at all is good and likes me well. Your arguments I can supplement with several others now. But still the glisten of fame on the distant peak from which my ideals look down on the rest of mankind, the brilliancy of genius, and the hope of catching for my own use some of their surplus glory have in it a wonderful attraction for me.

***

To Clarence Johnston, Oct. 25, 1879   **Cold Spring, N.Y.**

I will never forget, Clarence, when I deal with Englishmen, that I am dealing with a people who, at very best, are only our equals, whose praise may be regarded with complacency, whose rebuff may be regarded with serenity, and whose insult may be regarded with contempt. But this is away from the purpose and opposed to my intentions. In art all men are brothers; only in "style" are they at enmity. With the men I will associate . . . I will not be to them an American, but an artist. I will not carry with me national prejudice, but will never allow myself to forget national dignity. I go to learn, to acquire, to achieve; not as an intruder, but as a seeker after the things to be found nowhere else. . . .

If I can only experience some little of the opposition which is caused by honest difference of opinion and not be prejudice and conceit, it will force me to do better work and more of it, to improve my opportunities more, and to spur me on to <u>thought</u> rather than <u>exertion of present abilities</u>. . . .

My anxiety lies rather in the other direction, lest by too easy access to the "Goddess of Fortune" and favors unearned I should become all that is unprofitable, and should gain that pedantic self-importance which my nature so much inclines to.

I have had no time to sketch but I have managed to make a few scrawls of more or less importance. I find great interest in pencil and chinese-white as a medium for hasty and dashy—I may say also brilliant—sketching. . . .

***

Letter to Clarence Johnston, Nov. 17, 1879   **Cold Spring, N.Y.**

I sketch, I draw, I scrawl, I seldom think. My ideas become dulled from lack of use, my eye inapt for lack of training, and my fingers stiff from the careless attempt at careless objects. A cedar tree strikes my eye, I wish to sketch it; I sketch the trunk, the limbs I invent or horribly distort; and the foliage, well, that I generally "indicate." Yet my excuse is better than it seems at first sight. How can I sketch architecture when there is none to sketch? How can I study design—shall it be from the products of the carpenter's bench? How am I to think of color and form when the sunset is my only example of color and the rocks and trees are the only beautiful forms? . . .

No buildings here worthy of sketching, none worthy of criticism; no companions who know the least suggestion of artistic feelings. Yet still there lingers in my fingers the touches of design and beauty which I would long to express. . . . I designed some twenty factory office buildings of which one or two are sufficient as evidence of my depraved taste. . . .

I have not yet heard from Mr. Godwin, to whom I wrote, but expect a letter soon. If I don't get a favorable reply from him, I go to London without having secured a position. I go hopefully.

Letter to Clarence Johnston, Dec. 16, 1879   **New Lexington, Ohio**
I will return to Zanesville on Wednesday and on Monday next will go to Washington to present my letters of introduction and to obtain more. I have already a letter of introduction to the Consul at Liverpool (Mr. Packard of Louisiana), requesting him to give our letters to the Minister to England and the Consuls of various cities and especially to the Minister at Berlin. . . . I will have in money about $420.00 and the payment of my board until I am of age.

	3 Jan	Departure from New York
	17	Liverpool
	18	Chester
	20	London
	23	Southampton
	26	Salisbury, London
	29	Paris
	12 Feb	Turin
	13	Milan
	17	Venice
	22	Florence
	26	Rome
	6 Mar	Orvieto
	7	Siena
	10	Pisa
	11	Genoa
	13	Lyon
	20	Montbrison
	22	St. Antheme
	23	St. Amand
	24	Ambert
	26	Clermont
	28	Riom
	29	Gannat
	30	St. Porcain
	31	Moulins, Souvigny
	9 Apr	Nevers
	13	Bourges
	16	Orleans
	19	Clery
	20	Beaugency
	21	Mers, Chambord
	22	Blois
	26	Chaumont
	28	Tours
	30	Paris
	13 May	Chartres
	16	Paris
	22 Jun	Meru, Beauvais
	24	Amiens
	26	Rouen
	2 Jul	Serguigny, Lisieux
	3	Caen
	5	Honfleur
	6	Le Havre, London
	10	Cambridge
	11	London
	11 Aug	Ely
	13	Peterborough
	14	London
	ca. 1 Sep	Departure from Liverpool

Itinerary of Gilbert's 1880 grand tour

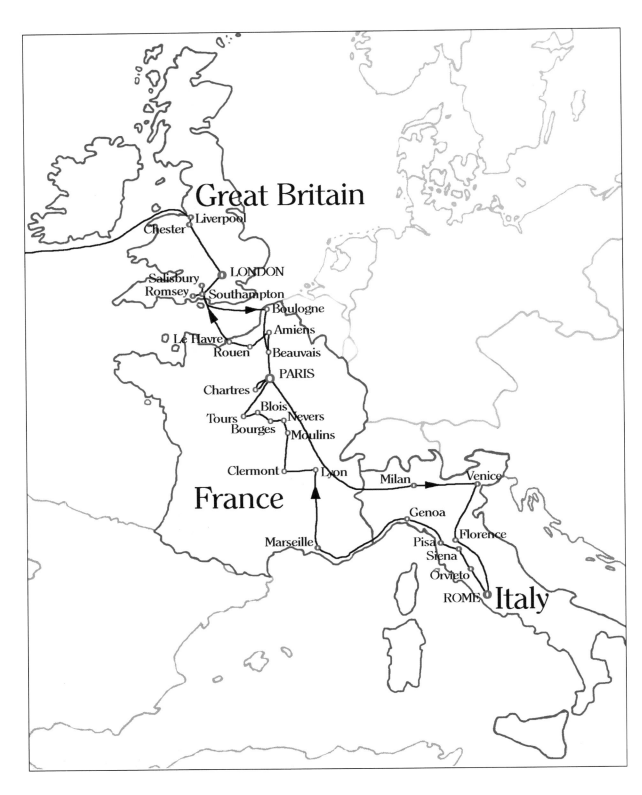

Route of Gilbert's 1880 travels in Europe

An English Preamble

To Elizabeth Gilbert, Jan. 18, 1880   **Angel Hotel, Liverpool**

When you all left the ship at New York, I went below and got my
state-room and my things secured and properly arranged so that
they could be found with the least possible trouble, took a dose of
"bromide of potas." (darn that stuff), and came on deck in a state of
"Ye who have tears, prepare to shed them now" sort of feeling and
mingled with the joyous host of 60 "weeping and teeth smashing"
travelers, as Beveridge would have said, who were going for pleasure
on a trip to Europe.

On deck I took my last look at New York about 4 o'clock, and as
we passed Coney Island I felt like a sailor. As the sun went down I
watched the fast disappearing sail of the pilot-boat and, muffling up
in my ulster, promenaded the deck in lonely glory.

I was as sick as I could be from the word go. . . . During my conva-
lescence I was more perfectly happy than I have ever been before
in my life, except once in Boston. I hadn't a care nor a sorrow,
I had not a pain, my mind was perfectly clear, and although I was
too weak to move I had a perfect joy in existence. My mind con-
jured up beautiful pictures and colors most vivid, and heretofore
by my unheard colors seemed read to my brush for use. Designs of
things of all sorts seemed at my fingers' ends, and cathedral spires,
domes, halls, and palaces seemed all to come at once to my mind
in forms more beautiful and grand than I had ever before seen them.
I must have had some species of delirium. . . .

I am at Angel Hotel. It seemed the most thoroughly English of all
the names mentioned and was said to be a moderately priced, quiet,
comfortable place where I would find no style and good living. It is
a queer place, surely, the most unlike a hotel of any hotel I ever saw.
It is not an inn, a tavern, a hotel, a boarding house, or any thing we
are accustomed to find in [the] United States.

I was received by a young woman who acted as clerk and made my terms with another one, a very lady-like person of about 30. My room was assigned me, my baggage carried up on the back of a porter, [my] trunk in the same way, and my fire built up by the servant maid. Now this all sounds like the reception we would get at the ordinary American house, but it was not like that. The manner of the people, the way they did things, and the quiet deliberation of their movements was, to a certain extent, charming.

Bed in Gilbert's room, Liverpool
Sketch in letter

My bed is high and hung with curtains, and my open fire place suggested comfort and the ingenuity of the designer at once. I have sketched it that you may understand the idea. And having sketched it, I think I need give no description. The principal point was that at the level of the top of the grate was a shelf on which could be placed articles which were to be kept warm. And then the flue was carried back of the main fire place so as to carry the flames and smoke away from the article heated. Back of the shelf the wall was coved (as in plan), and that threw additional heat out into the room. It was the most simply ingenious thing I have seen in a long time, and it goes down at once among the things to be remembered by me for future use.

Fireplace in Gilbert's room, Liverpool
Sketch in letter

The service at the table is very funny, and its solemn sensibleness outreaches description. If a man sees on another table what is not on his own, he goes over and helps himself, plate in hand, and returns satisfied, being quite polite about it. There is not the least offense, and it is even a pleasure to the man whose table is thus honored.

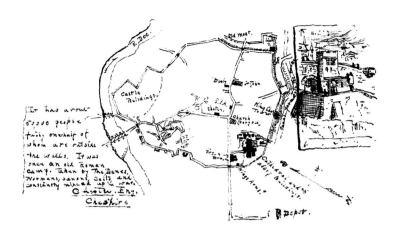

Plan of Chester
Sketch in letter

To Elizabeth Gilbert, Jan. 22   **The Green Dragon, London**

Tuesday afternoon I left Liverpool, and, having sent my portfolio on by express to London and invested in some fresh water-color, pencils, and sketch-books, I was in good condition to "do" Chester, as best it might be done in this season of the year. I was told by a very polite old gentleman on the cars about the hotels, and on his mentioning over the names of some I chose, as at Liverpool, for the name of the house instead of its modernness, and selected "The Green Dragon" as my inn. It is just inside the city gate and centrally located. I have sketched from memory the position of things and a view of one of the city gates. It is still well preserved and has much the look I have given it. The plan is like this, and as the walls are almost perfect in their original form, it is not difficult to picture medieval times with their plumed knights and armored troopers, the armies of the Earls of Derby and the Lords of Chester, [and] to hear "Marmion's" death-cry ringing from the walls. "Charge, Chester! Charge! On Stanley! On!" were the last words of Marmion. And to see in later times the gallant but routed host of King Charles as defeated under the walls of the city by Cromwell's men; they pass in haste and confusion through this very gate. . . .

View from Chester wall
Sketch in letter

Next we come to the castle. A grim, plain looking place, much modernized by a large new building. On the whole, the castle as seen from the walls doesn't impress me much except as a strong fortification and the seat of former Lords of Chester. As we pass around the castle walls (they run high above the city wall), we pass close to the River Dee. I have sketched it in pencil and will not speak further. Keeping on around the city walls, I found many queer places of similar nature to those already described and finally completed the circuit near "Kings Arms Kitchen" (an old "ale house" of Cromwell's time) and returned to the Green Dragon for a glass of ale and my supper.

I spent all morning in the cathedral. It is truly the most beautiful place I have ever been in. I am delighted with a water-color sketch I made of the interior of it, and am safe to say if I do no worse while I am abroad, I'll have no cause to be ashamed of my sketch-books. I made great friends with one of the "vergers" (named John Smith), and many was the legend he told and the nook of interest he pointed out to me as we went through the old place. He [was] inspired by my enthusiasm to exert himself.

Pew end at Chester Cathedral

Sketchbook 1, New-York Historical Society, negative 75216

To Elizabeth Gilbert, Jan. 24–28   Oaklands, Netley, Southampton

I left London about 9.00 A.M. in a dark and gloomy fog, everything shrouded in the uncertainty of mist, instead of the "mist of uncertainty," and with a general feeling of gloomy dampness pervading all objects. . . . I found Mr. Kirby waiting for me at the depot with a man-servant to carry my valise for me to the boat. . . . On the way down to the river, we passed a place where Watts lived once and where some of the finest hymns were written. . . . After looking over the boat, we went ashore at Woodestone and took a carriage for Netley Hospital and Netley Abbey.

Mr. Kirby's yacht at Southampton
Sketch in letter

Monday early we started for Romsey, where an old abbey is situated. We were here about an hour and left for Salisbury, where one of the most beautiful of all the Gothic cathedrals is situated. We were here about three hours, and most all the time was spent in the cathedral.

To Elizabeth Gilbert, Jan. 27, 1880   Golden Cross Hotel, London

This is the end of a most unsatisfactory and gloomy visit, not what I had anticipated would be one of the great places. . . . I find nothing in London what I had wished, and the climate is <u>most wretched</u>. . . . It is not only the fog that makes things bad, but when you think of the gases, odors, smoke, and foulness arising from a place of three million <u>inhabitants</u> . . . of architecture I can see <u>literally nothing</u>. . .

I am pleased with England and the people I have met, but am awfully disappointed in the general appearance of London. . . . The average appearance of the buildings is much lower than I had been led to expect from pictures. The Law Courts would form an inexhaustible supply of material for study, but the cold climate prevents such work. Westminster Abbey presents some remarkably beautiful interior detail, but the general effect of the interior does not excel Chester. The Parliament Buildings are, as far as possible,

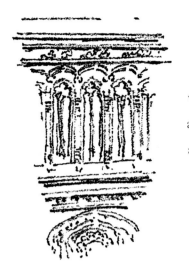

Triforium at Westminster Abbey
Sketch in letter

copies of Westminster and may be left out of consideration. The National Gallery is exceedingly fine in its display of paintings. The works of the present generation of architects, although worthy of the closest study, are so far apart and almost lost among the numerous buildings of mediocrity that more time would be wasted in finding them than it would pay to spend. To sum up, next fall if I can obtain a place in a first class office, one paid, I'll stay; if not, I'll take about two weeks more [in] London.

But from what I have seen of Chester, Salisbury, Netley, and Romsey, I feel more than satisfied that my visit to England had better be spent in the outlying towns and among the cathedrals. In the four places I have mentioned, I know many months could be spent with great pleasure and advantage.

I will start tomorrow morning by the South Eastern Railway for Paris, crossing from Folkestone to Boulogne and passing through Amiens on the way from Boulogne to Paris.

I will stop at Paris only a few days and will leave my trunk and portfolio there while I go on to Rome. I expect to be in Rome about a week and then go to Venice. Possibly I'll stop at Ravenna on the way to Florence; I'll be at Florence for a few days, and if my funds are in a good condition, I shall try to visit Naples. From Florence I'll send my valise back to Paris, and with a small satchel I have bought, slung over one shoulder, the field glass over the other, and my pockets stuffed with sketching materials, I'll walk through the south of France, guided by circumstances and the extent of my money. . . .

While in London I have presented my letters to Mr. Hoppin, Charge de Affaires of the American Legation, and to Mr. Cheney of the Gov't. Standards Office. From both I met a most cordial reception, especially from Mr. Hoppin, who is a splendid fellow and a very well informed man. Mr. Hoppin offers his services to gain me admission to places I could not visit without introductions and

Interior of Salisbury Cathedral from the choir
Library of Congress

has invited me to call on him socially as often as I feel inclined. Mr.
Cheney (Prof. Hilgard's friend) offers to introduce me to a celebrated
architect named Pierson and to Dean Stanley, also to gain admission
for me to the crypt and other unusual places for visitors at Westminster,

and to introduce me to the people at the Mint and at the Tower of London. I will avail myself of all these offers when I return.

To Clarence Johnston, Jan. 30, 1880   **Hotel du Bearn, Paris**

From Liverpool I went to Chester, the most serious and wonderful place I have ever seen. I was in Chester a day and a half and improved the time as best I could in sketching and sight seeing.

From Chester I went by way of Crewe, Rugby, and Lichfield to London, and on the way I was constantly surprised and delighted at the beauties and curiosities I saw. I passed Beeston Castle, of which I had a very good view. It was the ideal sort of thing, with battlements, turrets, a huge central tower, and a donjon keep, picturesquely interesting but of no architectural merit. As we neared Rugby I kept on the lookout for the schools, but the smoke and fog were so thick that I could see but a dim outline of the buildings.

Lichfield was the same way, and I was utterly unable to see a line of the cathedral. But as we passed Harrow (called Harrow-on-the-Hill) the air cleared a little, and I could see a bluish silhouette, a finely broken mass of buildings that I thought would make good subjects for study were time and clean air available. Near Harrow was an old ruined Early English church, and from this time on for a half an hour the country was dotted with many beautiful old churches of the Early English style, some in ruins and some sufficiently well preserved to be used for regular service. As we entered London we entered a veil of fog and mist such as I have never seen before and can not well describe. . . .

My impressions of London are of the misty kind, for from the time I arrived until I left, I was unable to see directly across the street. Nevertheless, I can fairly say I saw St. Paul's, Westminster, the Law Courts, Parliament Houses, Somerset House, Buckingham Palace, the Bank of England, Charing Cross, and Cleopatra's Needle. Besides these, there were many of the "Wren churches" and some very good modern store fronts. One of these latter in particular I remember and will sketch from

London storefront in the fog
Sketch in letter

memory. The beauty of it was its simple arrangement of forms; the mouldings were very flat and the carving was clear and sharp without being undercut. But the main thing I wanted to speak of was the repetition of design in the three stories of the building. Each story had over it a band of figures mighty well cut and well designed; the band was about 3'6" wide with plain fascias above and below about 8" wide. The window design was [illegible] throughout, and not a moulding was used where it could be dispensed with. . . . The simplicity of the design was a lesson to me. . . .

St. Paul's looked wonderfully big and had about as much architecture to it as the St. Paul Court House [in Minnesota]. There is, however, I must admit, a sort of grandeur in its size, and especially was this feeling forced upon one in the interior. I have seen much of Wren's work in London, and although seen in a hurry, I confess I haven't the slightest admiration for it.

Westminster also disappointed me as much as St. Paul's, for I had expected to see much more there. My first impressions of it are these (when I come to study it, they may be greatly changed): The nave has a gaunt, slender, hungry look, and every detail almost of the nave seems attenuated to the last degree. The nave seemed very dark and dingy, while the vaulting was only a roof of darkness. The transepts seem much more beautiful. Not having the extreme length of the nave they seem to gain in massiveness; and there being two very beautiful circular windows at each end of the transepts, the light is much better and the beautiful triforium shown with good effect. The piers and columns of the choir are much heavier and are ever so much handsomer than the piers of the nave and transepts. In the chapel is very wonderful vaulting, peculiar for its skill and ingenuity rather than its architectural beauty. The minor detail of this part of the abbey is very beautiful indeed, and it is really wonderful how much grace and feeling can be put into what we generally consider one of the most severe styles (the perpendicular). There were a whole lot of thin little columns and arches, about 40 in number, around one of the tombs; they were about a foot and a half high, and the detail was very minute and beautifully cut. The best part of Westminster is in the choir and the chapels, and I have promised myself a sketching season in that old place.

From London I gladly went to Southampton to visit Mr. Kirby, for I was used up by the fog. I met a warm welcome when I arrived at Southampton, and before going up to the house, and in order to use every minute of the time to advantage, we went around by Netley Abbey and the National Hospital. The Abbey is a very beautiful place; it is entirely in ruins and covered with ivy. The style was of the pure Early English and evidently all of one period. I had no time to sketch, but bought two 6 penny photographs, which I have just been looking for in vain. I had wished to sketch from the photographs for you.

In the wall of the abbey were many queer bits of flint and sea pebbles, and I was rather surprised to find whole oyster shells used in the joints and in filling the cracks of the facing. I suppose the surface was, in former times, covered with plaster and that shells were used as we use lath. . . .

Village church near Netley Abbey

Sketch in letter

Saturday afternoon was spent in taking a long walk to see the place, and on the way we stopped at a very old, curious little church, with transepts longer than the nave and a little bell tower up on the gable in the most audacious manner. It was built in very early times and has been altered frequently, having been used by allowing all the different sects that have won [favor] in England in the last 800 years.

From Netley early Monday morning Mr. Kirby and I started for Romsey and Salisbury. Romsey first: The tower is one of the real genuine kind—ancient, picturesque, and English to the last degree; quaint is no name for such places. We would not tolerate them in

Romsey Abbey
Sketch in letter

America; we love them in England. The abbey is the purest Norman work in England and in excellent preservation.

We were in Romsey about $3/4$ of an hour and I had time to make but one sketch . . . which I have reproduced here for you. It is just at the corner of the transept and nave, looking from the choir. The work is all very massive and has much of the detail we are accustomed to associating with Norman work. The interior is very light, and there is scarcely a particle of color to it except on the floor and in the choir. It is the color of the stones and the lack of stained glass that makes the whole effect. . . .

A very few minutes brought us to Salisbury (how thick these points of interest are). . . . Salisbury is a repetition of Romsey in all its quaintness and is perhaps even more interesting.

The Conciergerie

charcoal

Paris

Seine
Pont des Arts.

Paris in Haste

"a dealers"

Toymer

Gilbert

Views of Paris
Sketch in letter

Captivated by Paris

To Elizabeth Gilbert, Jan. 29, 1880   Postcard from Paris

I have been in Paris about 3 hours. . . . I am feeling first-rate in health and quite jolly.

To Clarence Johnston, Jan. 30, 1880   Hotel du Bearn, Paris

Here, at last, I am in the Mecca of the students of [the] Renaissance.

To Elizabeth Gilbert, Feb. 1, 1880   Hotel du Bearn, Paris

I wrote to you last Wednesday evening that I was about to leave London. I was literally driven off by the fog. I left there by the "tidal train," via Folkestone & Boulogne. . . . The channel was splendid, and the wind being from the southeast made the passage a very pleasant one. I have seen it rougher on Minnetonka. . . .

View of Boulogne from the English Channel
Sketch in letter

Boulogne presents a very fine appearance from the channel and has a general air of advancement and improvement, quite American. There is a very fine tower on a high hill near the harbor which makes the places have a finished architectural look, as though the whole composition were designed by one man. It is not infrequently the case with these foreign cities but seldom seen in America, and shows the vast improvement we might make by putting our prominent buildings in prominent places. . . .

Market in Paris
Library of Congress

On the car from Boulogne to Paris there was an Italian, a Frenchman,
a German, an English woman, and myself. We all got into conversation and had a great time. The Italian insisted upon it that I was
"Italiano," for he said I looked like one. The Frenchman could talk
all the languages and acted as interpreter. When I got to Paris I
found out why I looked like an "Italiano": My face still had the

remains of that London fog, so ground in that my complexion was that of a dirty organ-grinder. . . .

I take two meals a day and a cup of chocolate in the evening, so that my living costs me about $9.00 a week. This is beyond my means, I know, but I really can't live cheaper unless I live in a very poor way. . . .

Paris is kept as clean as a city can be kept and the streets are splendid. It reminds me greatly of Washington in the width and arrangements of the avenues, and of New York in the appearance of the shop fronts, only everything is much finer than in New York or Washington.

I have seen the Louvre and Tuileries, the Champs Elysees, the Trocadero (where the exhibition was held), the Place de la Concorde, the Colone Vendome, the Grand Opera House, l'Odeon, the Palais de Justice, La Sainte Chappelle, the "Arc du Triumphe," St. Sulpice

Notre Dame, Paris

Sketchbook 2, Library of Congress

Church, the "Chamber of Deputies," Cleopatra's Needle, "des Invalides," Ecole Militaire, and, the finest of all, Notre Dame. Notre Dame is simply without exception the most majestic and the most noble work of architecture I have ever seen. Chester with its simple dignity, Salisbury with its grace and beauty, Westminster with its gloom and solemnity —all are far surpassed by this building. Its towers are wonderful, its stained glass is gorgeous, its carving unequalled, its tracery of the most varied designs, all extremely beautiful, while the interior is the most thoroughly impressive that I can imagine.

There is no end of statuary and paintings, especially the first. Every building (almost) is covered with it, and on the Champs Elysees I counted 38 groups of marble and bronze figures, besides as many more vases and a number of fountains, all in a span about the size of an ordinary city square.

View from Gilbert's apartment in the Latin Quarter, Paris
Library of Congress

I had some trouble in finding Longfellow, but when I did find him, I met a most cordial and warm-hearted reception (Longfellow is Aiken's friend). . . . I found Chamberlain, Wilson, and Widdon, three American students all from the Ins. of Technology, and I was right at home at once. The atelier was in a perfect uproar when I entered, and it was the dirtiest place to study in I ever saw. Most of the fellows were smoking and all talking, laughing, or singing. I don't see how a fellow could study in such a place. Some of the young Frenchmen were exceedingly rude, and several had the impudence to join in the con-versation in French and then turn to me and make some high flow speech, gesticulating in a most stagey way. One young fellow was very smart and funny in French, and when he finished I replied in English, "I don't know just what you say, but I do know you are act-ing like a jack ass." He understood English, as did most of them, and blushed as red as a beet. He said no more but retired to his work.

I do wish I could stay here and study with them. They all live, as I do, in the famous Quartier Latin (Latin Quarter) and lead a mighty happy life.

It is much too cold to do outside sketching now in Paris, and I have decided to go on south at once. . . . I expect to be in Italy only about two weeks, for I must hasten on to the main work of this trip (the trip through Normandy). . . . By this time my money will probably be nearly all gone, and if I can't get the money from Cochran or get a position in London, I shall have to return to America. If Sammy could have my gun sold, I wish he would. I would take $50.00 for it if I could get it. He can have all he gets more than that. . . . I do wish I had somebody to travel with me; I get awfully sick of living alone and talking to myself.

I am filling my sketch-books and feel that every day I learn something that will be useful to me when I return.

To Elizabeth Gilbert, Feb. 6, 1880   **Hotel du Bearn, Paris**
Day before yesterday, I went to what is called "Hotel Cluny" on "Boulevard St. Germain." It is the remains of what has been used at different times for a Roman fort, Roman baths, a monastery, a palace, and a museum.

The Roman work is easily to be distinguished, and I could plainly
see what the different parts of the building had been used for. In the
Roman work, there were great round arches made of very small stones
and thin brick, many of the stones no bigger than our common bricks,
and the bricks as thin as our common floor tiles but broad and long.
Some of the arches were in a very ruined state, but all were well
enough preserved to show what massive effects they must have produced when perfect. There was one room that was unlighted by
windows and only reached by a narrow flight of stone stairs. It was

Unidentified old man
Sketchbook 2, Library of Congress

Hotel Cluny, Paris
Sketch in letter

down underground, and as I looked through the small doorway (see sketch) I thought I never had seen such a dismal hole. But the most of Hotel Cluny is in the late Gothic style (known in architecture as the Flamboyant), very beautiful in design and detail. The roof is almost as high as from the ground to the cornice of the building, and it is picturesquely broken up by chimneys, towers, and very beautiful dormer windows. Those old fellows never hesitated at carving and had no end of designs for gargoyles and tracery. I am making a special study of gargoyles so that I may be able to use lots of them when I get to work.

I made a water-color sketch of the courtyard of Hotel Cluny, but it is not altogether satisfactory, for being made in cold weather when my fingers were stiff I could not attempt much.

In the gallery of the Louvre I have seen some real "old masters": Raphaels, Michelangelos, Titians, Tintorettos, Correggios, Rubenses, Van Dycks, Rembrandts, and lots more which I can't remember, and, in the Palace of the Luxembourg, the finest works of modern artists in France. And now, to tell the honest truth, I think I like the works of the modern school far better than the ancient. That is, in painting; in sculpture and architecture, of course, it is different.

The shops and stores are wonderfully interesting to me, and many a time I find myself staring in at the window of some dry-goods store in admiration of the gaudy, brilliant colors. I often want to buy a few yards of the rich and beautiful material, just to hang around my room to look at, as I would a picture.

Gilbert's copy of a sketch by Viollet-le-Duc of his work on Notre Dame, Paris
Library of Congress

Lots of times I go into a store and spend an hour looking over photographs of cathedrals and medieval towers and end in buying a one franc view of some celebrated place of interest.

This part of Paris is almost entirely inhabited by students and is the greatest place you ever saw. I have been in the rooms of many of them, and they are a jolly, hospitable, warm hearted set, reckless and careless to the last degree, and spending two thirds of their last franc for pleasure. One fellow I have met, a painter, was down to his last sou a week ago when a medical student got a remittance and gave him an order for a portrait. The money was paid in advance, and nothing would do but the painter must give a dinner to his friends immediately.

Nor is there any aristocracy of wealth or birth in the Latin Quarter. Every man is what his work makes him, and it is only an utter boor that is not received with open arms.

I'll leave my portfolio with Longfellow. I take with me my black overcoat, my heavy shoes, a change of linen, and underclothes; I will wear my brown suit and carry my things in a small satchel I bought in London (it is black with nickel trimmings [and] will be slung over my shoulder). I have bought a pair of leggings for walking to save my pants. They are brown canvas trimmed with leather and buckled down the sides. My watch and a common iron chain and my ring are all the jewelry I'll carry so as not to tempt robbers.

[text missing] . . . such a lot of time that it is almost impossible to sketch. I do not begrudge the time and labor, but I feel as though I had better learn while I can and be able to carry back as much knowledge as I can instead of trying to send my knowledge on ahead of me.

Bridge at the Public Garden, Venice

A Whirlwind through Italy

In the weather I have been most unfortunate since I came to Europe.
Five-sixths of the time it has been either foggy, rainy, or very damp and
cloudy. . . . I think it has been my great enthusiasm for the wonders of
the old Gothic architecture that has kept me satisfied. Certainly if I
had been traveling for health or pleasure alone, I would have given up
in despair before this. . . .

I don't know what I am going to do if I can't save some way. At this
rate, I will be on my way home before the last of July, and unless I can
sell my water-colors, write, or get a place in a London office, I am
afraid my visit will be shorter than I had expected. . . .

I have tried several times to write a letter to some American paper,
but each time the attempt has been a failure; my thoughts are frozen
the moment I try to write anything interesting or newsy. But when I
start to writing to you or any of my friends, my thoughts come so fast
that they are put down in hurried sentences (and misspelled words)
as rapidly as I can write. . . .

The principal thing to see in Milan is, of course, the cathedral.
I can easily see how to the mind unused to considering the architectural qualities of a building it would have a most striking effect.
It is of late date and mixed style, having much classic detail on the
main facade and the interior. It is built of beautiful marble, which
has assumed many tints and shades of rich yellow and light pinkish
grey. . . . There is none of the broad massiveness of Notre Dame,
nor the graceful elegance of Salisbury Cathedral, but there is an
amount of skill and lavish ingenuity in the workmanship of the
detail that is truly wonderful. The skyline is a wilderness of pinna-
cles and flying buttresses, carved and moulded to the last extreme.
I never saw anything to compare with it in lavish, almost barbaric
luxuriousness. . . .

Foscari Palace, Venice

Sketchbook 1, New-York Historical Society, negative 75217

The vaulting seemed most wonderful: a mass of tracery, delicate, intricate, almost fairy-like, it seemed. But ah! Here is a disappointment, here is unpardonable deception. An impossibility achieved, and how? But trickery. A large flake of the tracery had dropped out at some previous period, and the laths showed through. I was disgusted to think what an enthusiastic ass I had been to be even for a moment so

56

deceived. From the moment I saw that the vault was plastered and the tracery unreal, I looked at everything suspiciously. . . .

I bought a number of photographs of Milan Cathedral and a few of the city. I never saw such photographs, and so wonderfully cheap. . . .

[letter recommenced Feb. 19 in Venice]

At last I am in Venice: City of poetry, art, and romance. Home of Titian, Tintoretto, Canova, Byron, Enrico Dandolo Cabot, the Foscari, and a thousand other names not less famous.

Ah! This is the place to live in, this land of Italy and this city of Venice. A mighty funny place, full of interest, very quaint, very beautiful. A lovely place. Every day I find myself among things of ancient times. Today as I sat by the Grand Canal and sketched the facade of the Foscari Palace, I almost imagined myself an ancient Venetian and that the swiftly gliding gondolas bore the dignitaries of state and the nobles of the ruling city of the world. It does not seem strange to me to be sketching the Foscari Palace and to be wandering among the relics of the ancient splendor of a great people, for Venice really was at one time the greatest city of the world.

But to return: I left Milan at 12.20 P.M. on Tuesday (still in a fog). We hurried through a level country, ditched and hedged and cultivated in a thrifty, scientific way. . . . I will read up in the guide-book some time of the things I passed between Milan and Venice, but at present my recollection of them is somewhat indistinct. I do remember one very large and massive fortress near Verona and another near Solferino; and then there were the greatest number of campaniles, always two or three in sight, sometimes a half a dozen and more. I keep constantly at hand a small note book for sketches from the car window, and I was enabled to get some few sketches of the buildings as we stopped at the station.

At Vicenza (pronounced in Italy "Vechen-sah") I got quite a sketch of an old tower, but it was, of course, very rough and hasty.

I arrived in Venice about 9.30 P.M. and gave myself up to the tender mercies of the "commissionaire" of the Hotel Victoria as soon as I could find him. He found me a gondola and off I went for the hotel. It was the queerest thing to ride in I have ever seen. Very pleasant, easy, no jolting, and soft cushions to lie back on. . . . My gondolier could turn a corner and come within 2 inches of the wall every time and not touch it. He seemed to have such perfect control over the boat that in a little while it was rather an amusement to mentally bet that he would come within a given distance of some object ahead.

Gondola on the Grand Canal
Sketch in letter

A gondola is about 30 ft. long (and all are the same size), about 5 ft. broad, and the covered part is high enough to sit up in and have plenty of head room. The inside of the cab is cushioned with very large, soft cushions, all in black, and hung with curtains and fringes. The side lights are of glass; like a railroad car window they may be raised or lowered at pleasure. In the door is the same arrangement, so that the damp winds of the Adriatic may be kept out. They are some of them elaborately carved all over and most of them carpeted, but none except omnibuses painted in colors other than the most somber black. . . .

We came to a large palace then, under a bridge, and as we shot out from under its dark arch, the Bridge of Sighs was just ahead. We passed under the Bridge of Sighs, and Byron's lines came to mind quite vividly:

> "I stood in Venice on the Bridge of Sighs,
> A palace and a prison on each hand,
> I saw from out the wave her structures rise,
> As from the touch of the Enchanter's Wand."

. . . Venice is one of the most interesting places I have seen, and may be ranked with Chester and Salisbury in England as a well preserved specimen of an ancient city. St. Mark's, of course, is the great thing in Venice to see. . . . The guide told me that

Bridge of Sighs
Sketch in letter

Campanile of San Marco, Venice
Library of Congress

Interior of San Marco, Venice

Library of Congress

the mosaics of St. Mark's needed constant repairing and occasionally pieces dropped out from the vaults above. It was an accidental remark, but the idea instantly came into my head that I would haunt the neighborhood until I got a few small pieces. They are made of stone and of some composition the secret of which is a lost art. They are at least a thousand years old and were brought from the neighborhood of Constantinople.

For about an hour I walked up and down the cloisters, looking for a few small pieces, but in vain. At best it would be only a matter of luck, and I concluded to leave it entirely to chance. I got my water-colors and sketch-book and started a somewhat bold attempt at the interior of St. Mark's. It is one vast mosaic of gold, studded with Bible history and monastic legends in the most brilliant mosaics. It is one of the most remarkable interiors in Europe, not so very large nor so very high, but of the most brilliant color. A complete study of interior decoration. It is not more beautiful than Trinity Church interior in Boston, but much more brilliant, for the surface of gold reflects every ray of sunlight a thousand times.

As I sat and sketched and studied, I heard a sharp rattle on the floor behind me, then another as though some one had dropped a marble on the pavement. I jumped up and there, right behind me, were a few small pieces of mosaics on the pavement. They had just fallen. What luck. Almost phenomenal. I picked up 6 pieces in all and one a gold one. My delight exceeded all bounds. . . . I would not take $5.00 apiece for them. I am going to give one piece to Clarence, two to the Ins. of Technology, and keep three myself. I consider it a most wonderful thing that I have gotten these little things, for their historic, artistic, and architectural interest is very great. The pieces are irregular in shape and of dark red and brown colors, about so large. They will be the greatest trophy of this trip, I am sure.

I got quite a satisfactory sketch of St. Mark's and felt in a good humor with all mankind when I left for the hotel.

In Venice the second day at breakfast I became acquainted with a gentleman from Washington, D.C., a medical student at Vienna and a practicing physician at home. He is about 30 years old, a very pleasant

fellow, and a gentleman, apparently. He proposed that we hire a guide
for the day and get a gondola together. . . . Since then we have been
almost constantly together and will probably keep together until we
get through Rome. His name is Dr. S. B. Lyon. I was in Venice from
Tuesday night until Sunday noon and was able to sketch a good deal
in that time. My visit there was one of exceedingly great interest and
one I will always like to remember. The relics I brought away are some
plaster from the Bridge of Sighs, my mosaics, some very excellent
photographs, a pair of small mosaic cuff buttons, and a very little
cheap shell-work made by a gondolier's child.

To Elizabeth Gilbert, Mar. 4   **Rome**

Dr. Lyon and I had a bully time in Florence. . . . The first day we visited the Chapel of the Medicis, where several cardinals and many
princes of this celebrated family lie. Here also are those wonderful
works of Michelangelo, "Night and Day," "Dawn and Evening." . . .
Nothing that I could say would be sufficient praise for them. But I
can't go into detail of all that I saw in Florence or this letter will not
be written before I sail for home. From the Chapel of the Medicis we
went to the Uffizzi Gallery (pronounced U-fit-se), and as we went up
the grand stairway I innocently asked, "Are there any of the Uffizzi
family alive now?" When you know that "Uffizzi" means office-holders
and that the Uffizzi Palace means the Governmental Office Building,
you will see the enormity of the joke. . . .

[letter recommenced ca. Mar. 8 in Siena]

From the Uffizzi there is a passage way over a half a mile long to the
Pitti Palace. . . . The sides of it are hung full with engravings, studies,
sketches, cartoons, and tapestries from works by the old masters. . . .
I saw an ancient engraving of Penn's treaty with the Indians by
Michelangelo. Also the signing of the Declaration of Independence
by the same author, a sketch for a centennial exposition building by
Giotto, and several competitive designs by Raphael for the decoration
of the interior of the Washington Monument. . . .

[letter recommenced ca. Mar. 14 in Lyon]

Tower of Palazzo Vecchio, Florence

National Museum of American Art, Smithsonian Institution

Bell tower on the Piazza della San Annunziata, Florence
Library of Congress

In the afternoon we took in the church of Santa Croce, the Duomo, Baptistry, and Giotto's campanile, San Annunziata, and a painter's studio. This made a pretty good day, but nevertheless it was still light and I got my sketch-book and made the next hour profitable. . . .

Quite early the next morning we started out for the Carthusian Monastery of Chartreuse . . . one of the old stopping places of the crusades. . . . It is most beautifully situated on the crest of a hill whose slopes are covered with olive and almond trees. . . .

A pleasant looking monk came out to meet us. He never bothered his stomach with fasts, nor disturbed his rest with midnight vigils, I'll bet. But he was a jolly good fellow and very polite. I was shown the Campo Santo, or burying ground. It is a little flat of ground not more than 40 feet wide and 80 long, but for generations past the monks have been buried there. They are dumped right in without any coffin and lime thrown over them to assist in the decomposition, and the earth thrown over them and smoothed down as before. No mark or stone is put up, but their bones "mingle in death as their souls will in —," as the doctor said. Their cells are very comfortable places, indeed. Each monk has a bed room and a small sitting room, a tiled or brick floor, a little front porch, a small garden patch, a place in the basement for tools, and quite a large balcony on the outer wall of the monastery. . . .

There is an awful lot of nonsense about monks generally, but this monastery is such a clean, well preserved, and comfortable one that when I join the Roman Catholics, I am going there. . . . They are, as a general thing, a great benefit to the neighborhood, and the erroneous idea I had, that they made the people poor and squalid, is quite corrected.

The second day in Rome, the Doctor came around and we made arrangements to go out together early the following morning. I spent the day in a visit to the Forum, the Palace of the Ivirinal [?], the Princian Hill, a mosaic manufacturer, and a water-color picture store (for I wanted to freshen up my mind on water-colors and there is no place like Rome for good water-color pictures). In the Forum I saw the temple of Antoninus & Faustina, the School of Xanthus, the Temple of Castor & Pollux, the Temple of Peace or the Basilica of Constantine, the arch of Septimus Severus, the Arch of Titus, the rostrum from

Temple of Castor and Pollux in the Forum, Rome

Library of Congress

which Cicero used to speak, the Column of Phocas, the Cloaca Maxima, and many ancient ruins and remains. The whole place is filled with fragments of capitals, columns, cornices, mouldings, and all the different parts that used to make up the beauty of an ancient Roman's idea of architecture. . . .

Now I am commencing to get mixed up as to just when I visited all these places, but I know I saw them and retain a clear idea of their appearance. But I do remember having visited the Colosseum by moonlight and a noble sight it was. . . . As I entered it the first time, with the full moon rising behind its farther walls and casting strange lights and black shadows on the surrounding objects, all the associations of the place seemed so grand that I involuntarily took off my hat with a feeling almost of awe.

The first day Dr. Lyons and I went out together, we went first to St. Peter's, climbed up into the ball, and saw the Mediterranean and half of Italy through a window which is invisible from below. We visited during the day the Rospigliosi Gallery, the Colonna Gallery, Corsini Gallery, St. John Lateran . . . [and the] Villa Borghesi, where I saw the King and Queen. . . .

The second day we were out together we visited the Palace of the Caesars, the Palace of Nero, the Baths of Titus, the Baths of Caracalla, the Houses of Somebody-or-other, the Columbarium, the Catacombs, the Tomb of Cecilia Mettella, Tomb of Seneca, the House of Reingi, the Arch of Janus, the Temple of Vesta, the Forum of Trajan, the Theatre of Marcellus, and lots more that don't come readily to mind. In the evening the Doctor and I parted in hopes of a "meeting" in the better land, as he pathetically said. He was going to Naples and I must henceforth tread my weary way alone. I can't resist the temptation to sketch the Doctor as he sadly yet calmly gazed upon an erring guide that had told us the same lie twice about different places.

Dr. S. B. Lyon
Sketch in letter

Baths of Caracalla, Rome

National Museum of American Art, Smithsonian Institution

After this I went around alone, and it is out of the question for me to think of mentioning the places I visited during the following week. Suffice it to say I have seen the finest galleries of paintings the world has to show, the most perfect sculptures that ever were made, the rarest monuments of antiquity. The paintings of all the old masters, most of the churches of Rome, Michelangelo's "Moses," Guido's "Beatrice Cenci" and his "Aurora," Raphael's "Transfiguration," the Sistine Chapel, the Pope, the Cardinals, the whole of St. Peter's, many palaces. . . .

I can hardly take time to mention how, while sketching the Porta San Paolo on the outskirts of Rome, I was able to assist two American ladies who were lost; and with them visited the tombs of Shelley and Keats. How I met a fellow student from the Ins. of Technology under the dome of St. Peter's. How I made the acquaintance of an American artist in the Forum while sketching there. How I visited some excavations, crawled into an old vaulted passage just unearthed and found some bits of pottery and a few old bronze coins which I shall some day take great pleasure in showing you. . . . I was in Rome about 10 days and the whole time was one continued excitement and hurry. It was a busy time which I shall never forget. I guess I saw more in ten days than most people see in a month, and I did some sketching too.

I left Rome early Sunday morning for Orvieto. . . . It is at the top of a mountain and overlooks the country for miles. A river winds through the valley far below the city and adds great charm to [the] view. It is just such a place as an artist would delight to paint, and is just the place we imagine when we think of Utopia and Arcadia. . . .

There is a very beautiful cathedral at Orvieto of white marble inlaid with exceedingly rich mosaics that glitter and glow with a dazzling light in the warm southern sun and under the blue sky of Italy. The narrow, crooked streets, the bold, strong, simple architecture, the sudden turns revealing some beautiful work, some old window or ancient doorway, or some beautiful view of the valley and the hazy mountains far away, the cheerful, happy, healthy, honest looking people in their quaint costumes, the donkeys loaded with bundles of wood or paniers of vegetables go to make up a most charming picture.

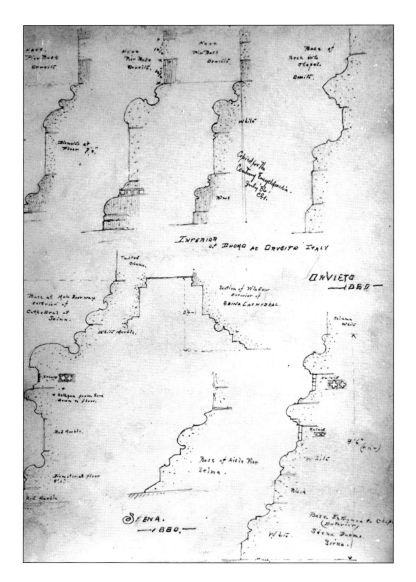

Moulding profiles in Orvieto and Siena

Sketchbook 1, New-York Historical Society, negative 75219

Ah: surely I will never forget a day of this wonderful journey that opens up to me new sights of beauty every hour I live and every place I visit. . . . I was in Orvieto only two half days and one night. Wouldn't have missed it for anything. I reached Siena at 4.30 the same afternoon. In fifteen minutes from the time I landed, I was out sketching. . . . Siena is about the medium between Florence and Orvieto in size, importance, activity, and beauty. There is the best decorative iron work I have ever seen, all over the city. . . .

I was in Siena over two nights and one day and hurried to Pisa. I went right up to the Duomo, Baptistry, and Leaning Tower. I saw the whole thing in a short time. The Baptistry is quite a beautiful thing and there is a wonderful echo in the interior. The Duomo is of that debased style which afflicts so many of the buildings of this part of Italy and which is

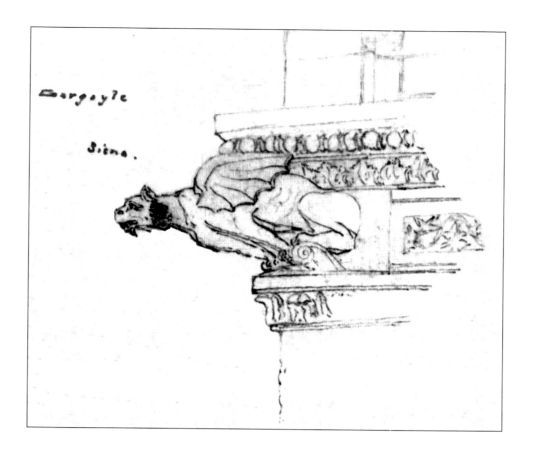

Gargoyle, Siena Cathedral
Sketchbook 1, New-York Historical Society, negative 75220

so lauded by guide-books and tourists, to my intense disgust. The
Leaning Tower is a great curiosity and not without some beauty. . . .
I stopped to sketch the baptistry and missed my train. . . . The
ride from Pisa to Genoa was rather disagreeable. The people in the car
all smoked the vilest tobacco, and I think if there is one thing
I hate worse than the "old scratch," it is bad tobacco. Fully 3/4 of the
way was underground. I never saw so many tunnels in my life all put
together. We were running most of the way right up to the shore of
the Mediterranean Sea. . . .

To Elizabeth Gilbert, March 10, 1880   **Postcard from Pisa**
Will keep writing cards to you every day. My sketchbook is filling up
rapidly, and in that respect the trip has been very profitable.

To Elizabeth Gilbert, March 13, 1880   **Postcard from Marseilles**
Weather is simply splendid. Almond trees in blossom and orange

The Italian Mediterranean coast
Sketch in letter

groves full of fruit. The whole way was right on the shore of the Mediterranean, sometimes high up on the side of the mountains so that the sea seemed under us.

Scene in Italian village
Library of Congress

Sailboats on the Mediterranean

Sketchbook 1, New-York Historical Society, negative 75227

Church at Tours

National Museum of American Art, Smithsonian Institution

Along the Rhone and the Loire

I arrived in Marseilles about 8.30 the next morning after having travelled all night, in fact, from Genoa the day before. I only stopped at Ventiniglia long enough to have my satchel examined by the custom-house and get my ticket for Marseilles. I got my mosaics through all right, undiscovered, and rejoiced accordingly. I washed up and got breakfast at Marseilles and took the next train for Lyon. I had passed by Monaco, Nice, Mentone, and a host of beautiful places to hurry on to what will be the main work of this trip. I entirely skipped my programme from C. Retiniglia to Marseilles, and now that it is passed I feel that I have made a sacrifice in a good cause and am glad of it.

On the way from Marseilles to Lyon, we were running the whole way in the valley of the Rhone by handsome towns and pretty villages. The country is well cultivated and the scenery has a sensible, quiet look, distantly reminding me of the valley of the Minnesota River. . . . I should like to have stopped at Avignon, for from the car window I could see some beautiful towers and the old cathedral, with its huge flying buttresses and recessed windows, as charming as all cathedrals are, with the added beauty of distance and association with bygone times, when Reinzi came a pilgrim to its shrine.

If ever I come to France again, I have put down in my programme at least a week in Avignon. We passed another very pretty little place called "Isle." If ever I can see a picture of it, my last centime goes but what that picture is mine. . . .

The money I have will be sufficient to last me until the 15th of May unless some unforeseen circumstance happens. If my applications in London are successful, I will go there at once and stay until I have replenished my pocket book and then take a tour through Normandy in the summer and my walk in England in the autumn.

Notre Dame Cathedral, Montbrison
Library of Congress

I have written a 14 page letter to "Scribner Magazine." My subject is
"the present condition of Italy." They can't any more than refuse the
article, and that much might be done by any paper. If they accept it,
I'll be so much the better off. It is better to aim high than not to aim
at all. If the article is rejected, I have asked them to forward it to you,
saying you would pay the postage. If they send it to you, will you please
look it over? And if you think it worthy, revise it a little and send it
with out a word or comment to the "Pioneer Press," only requesting
it be returned to our post office box if unused.

I have written to the "American Architect & Building News," offering
them sketches of my trip free of charge. If the sketches are accepted,
they will give me an established footing among our draughtsmen and
architects that will enable me to more easily find a good position
and fair salary when I return. If they are rejected, I have asked that
they be left in Mr. Ware's care until I return. . . .

It has seemed as if this letter never would be written, for abbreviate it
as much as I could, it has been impossible to make it shorter. I know
you will excuse all errors and ill-formed sentences (lead-pencil as well),
for written as such a letter must be, when ever time was to be had, and

often in a whirl of excitement and in the fatigue of travel, it would need several rewritings and many corrections to make it anything like a sensible composition.

To Elizabeth Gilbert, March 20, 1880   Postcard from Montbrison

I sketched the Cathedral of Montbrison this morning, and as there is nothing else of interest here, I will walk over to St. Antheme.

To Clarence Johnston, March 21, 1880   Montbrison

Constant travel and an excited brain (never given to any deep or protracted course of thought, at best) have had much to do with my not writing. . . . So it has been until I have at last a quiet Sunday in this little old town in central France. . . .

I send these letters just as they were left unfinished, and when they abruptly break off, you must supply in your imagination what I was about to say. From Rome I went to Orvieto, from Orvieto to Siena, from there to Pisa, from Pisa to Genoa, and from Genoa to Lyon. Lyon is one of the best places I have been to yet, and although almost my whole time was spend in letter writing, I found time to sketch the design of a traceried spire and some ancient iron hinges.

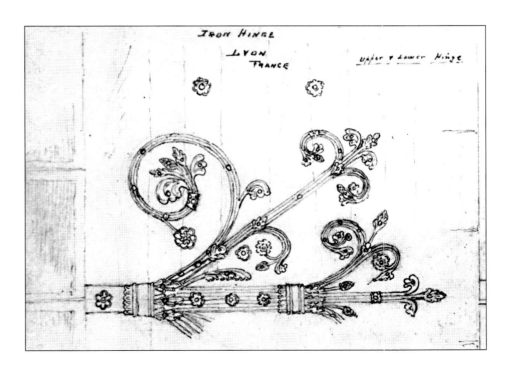

Detail of iron hingework on door in Lyon

Sketchbook 1, New-York Historical Society, negative 75221

Church at St. Antheme

Library of Congress

From Lyon I came to Montbrison, and from here I start early tomorrow morning toward Clermont. I will get to St. Antheme by night and in the morning push on, sketching by the way and living a merry life on foot from town to town until I get again the neighborhood of rail-roads. My costume is unique and quite serviceable, not to say artistic.

I have a light gray hat of English
make, flexible and soft with visors
both before and behind, a brown
suit of clothes that is exactly the
thing for this sort of a tour, and a
pair of light brown canvas leggings
to protect my pants from wear,
dust, and mud. My sketch-books,
guide-book, and sketching stool are
done up in a short strap, and a
change of underclothes with qui-
nine, pencils, a flask of brandy, and my
water-colors are in a small satchel slung
over my shoulder.

"Our Special Artist" veiwing the Promised land.

Gilbert on his way to Clermont
Sketch in letter

When I get down to business, I calculate to average walking 20 miles
a day; at present 12 miles will be quite sufficient. My walk tomorrow
is 13 miles. I will visit Clermont, Moulins, and Nevers, then strike
for Orleans, Chartres, Blois, Tours, and on toward Normandy.

To Elizabeth Gilbert, March 22, 1880   Postcard from St. Antheme
I had some jolly adventures this morning [while walking from
Montbrison to St. Antheme]. Was arrested by the Mayor of Verierre,
who took me for some sort of a spy. I had no passport, and only the
most consummate cheek got me off. That fellow was a rascally idiot.
I will go as far as Ambert tomorrow, perhaps as far as St. Armand.

The roads are splendid, and if I get tired walking, there is almost
always a "diligence" handy. There is a charming old country church
here which I am going out to sketch after dinner.

To Elizabeth Gilbert, March 22, 1880   St. Antheme
Early this morning I left Montbrison on the first real walk of this
tour. Leggings on and good roads before me, I felt confident of a
pleasant day. I had scarcely got out of Montbrison before I took the
wrong road. This one mistake led me into some curious adventures
and over much rough country. . . . I came to a queer old ruin high

Tower of church at Ambert

Sketchbook 1, New-York Historical Society, negative 75223

up on a crag, at the foot of which was a little old church. It was a strangely pleasant place, and I wandered around among the lizards and ivy vines a few minutes, trying to make up my mind to sketch the thing, but suddenly, thinking of my day's walk ahead, I started to find my way again. . . .

Talk of France being a free democratic country: It's no such thing; it is the most despotic sort of a government. The people haven't the first idea of free action (in traveling). Italy is comparatively civilized, England is quite so, but France is way back in the Middle Ages as compared with America. Every petty mayor, street-scavenger, policeman, or custom house officer has some little authority which he must show on every occasion. . . . Yet the peasants and the ordinary people are very kind and pleasant and will do most anything for one. . . .

At just noon I came on to the main road, which I should have taken at Montbrison, and a sharp hour's walk brought me into St. Antheme. It is only a small place, but there is a picturesque church here (which I sketched this afternoon) and some queer houses. I shall go on to Ambert in the morning, where I'll stay over night, though if I get there in good time, I may push on to St. Armand. I enjoy this sort of life immensely, and as I go from place to place, sketching the good things and hurrying on, I feel as if I were enjoying an opportunity seldom to be gotten by an American draughtsman. . . .

[letter recommenced Mar. 25 at Ambert]

I thought I would try to get to Ambert rather than be blocked in at St. Antheme by bad roads or continued rainstorms. My road led me right through the mountains, and although the road was most excellent, there was a great pine forest on one side and a steep rocky mountain on the other. It was about as lonely a walk as I care to take.

At one point in the road I was at the dividing line of two watersheds. . . . The valley behind me was all black with the coming storm and dismal pines crowned the hills; the valley ahead was lit up by sunshine, the slopes green with young grass and wheat; and the white-walled red-roofed cottages of the peasants took the place

Scene in Auvergne
Library of Congress

of the great dismal moss-grown crags I had just passed. Ambert, with
its quiet streets and great church tower, lay snugly down in the valley
near a little river. . . .

Ambert is a lovely place. It is just such a place as would "fit" in a story.
It is very clean: lots of fresh water, some of the streets wide, with here
and there an open square, yet enough narrow streets with those queer
old houses which over hang the street a yard or more at every story,
and then end up with great projecting cor-
nices which almost touch each other across
the street. The church of the parish is really
ideal. It has a noble Norman tower with
buttresses and gargoyles to the heart's con-
tent, and to crown all there is running up
from one corner of it the most charming turret I ever saw.

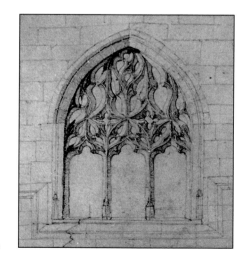

I am the most conspicuous figure in Ambert,
I do believe. The boys have taken a great
fancy to my sketching stool, for it excites
the greatest curiosity and amusement. It is

*Flamboyant Gothic window
at Ambert Cathedral*
Sketchbook 1, New-York Historical Society, negative 75222

the funniest place to sketch in. Everybody wants to see what I am doing, and as a general thing they crowd around so close as to bother me. When matters get quite bad, there is always some choleric old fellow with a staff (and wooden shoes) who assumes control of matters, takes the best position to look over my shoulder, and swears vehemently if any one jostles my elbow or gets in between me and my object. If swearing don't act quick enough, the staff is a gentle persuader, or if it is not long enough, off comes . . . the "sabot," which flies with unerring aim at the offender's head. I never saw such curious people. They are more good natured than in the valley of the Rhone and much better to deal with. Many words in their "patois" are the same as our English words, and when I speak in Parisian I am less understood than when I use a mixture of English and Italian. . . .

Few artists travel through this part of France, and the people scarcely know what to make of a fellow that sketches and loafs about; and that a gentleman should travel on foot is far beyond their comprehension. . . .

In Italy, Americans are not thought much of; and, indeed, in many parts of France we are much underrated, but here as in England they think more of us. By the way, I may say right here that, although mortifying to our national pride, the United States is not regarded by the peoples of Europe, so far as I have had an opportunity to find out, with the respect as a nation which it should have.

All day yesterday was spent in sketching and also was today, for I have found this a most profitable place to visit.

I have concluded to take the "diligence" tomorrow for Clermont, for as the road between here and there is very mountainous and not thickly populated it had better be passed by. . . .

I often imagine myself coming back here or to any of the places I visit, with some friend or you. . . . I have lost none of the enthusiasm which I had on first visiting such places, but each town calls forth some new thoughts and shows me some new delight. Things seem just as queer, just as "Utopian," and just as beautiful in each separate place. And the quiet enjoyment of such things as I see makes me more thoughtful and gives me a contented feeling for every discomfort I may encounter.

Every day I have reason to think that I am one of the most favored of mortals, for I wander perfectly free from care and at my own will, the whole time one peaceful, splendid holiday. How different from the excited, hurried, ambitious, feverish life I led just a year ago; yet I am learning just as much as then. I am learning to live, and to see beauty in everything.

To Elizabeth Gilbert, Mar. 28, 1880   Hotel Puy de Dome, Riom

The diligence ride from Ambert to Port de Dore on the way to Clermont was very interesting. . . . We changed horses every five miles and drivers once in 15 miles, and as I had a seat in the front of the "diligence," I could watch the operation. The horses as a general thing are small and as bony as a sunfish, but a few big Normandy horses occasionally are seen, and the farther west I get, the more frequent they become.

The diligence was one of the two-story kind and had two compartments below. The compartment in front was entered over the wheel; the one behind was accessible by a pair of steps that swung from the rear in a dangerous way. The upper story was reached by a ladder or by climbing a pair of steps near the driver's seat, a rope, or strap swung by these steps to assist in the ascent, and it afforded me much amusement on the way to tie the end of the whip to this strap when the driver wasn't looking and watch his next attempt to lash the horses. The driver's seat was clear out over the horses so that he could see everything. There were two tongues to this wonderful vehicle, and the horses were driven three abreast a la Wagner's "Chariot-Race." . . .

I have sketched the "diligence" as it lay at Oliargues (can you pronounce it?), waiting for the horses for the next stage. . . .

A diligence in Auvergne

Sketch in letter

Clermont Cathedral is one of the very large cathedrals of the country, although not especially celebrated or very beautiful. The nave is very high and long, and all the details are such as to add to the effect of height and length. Everything has a wiry, attenuated appearance disagreeable to my eye, reminding me of the most disagreeable features of Westminster Abbey. The piers are clusters of columns, of course, but the columns are so slender as to look almost like reeds. When a column six inches in diameter runs up sixty feet or more with out break or moulding of any kind, even though it be surrounded by others similar to itself, it is going a little too far to suit my taste. . . .

I am glad I visited it, for I think I learned more from its bad features, as warnings, than had it been a really good thing. . . .

Today I walked from Clermont to Riom through Montferrand. Riom is a good enough place to stay over night in, but has little that would pay to sketch. However, there is a fine Gothic chapel, a Romanesque church, and two others of mixed style, all containing good suggestions. . . .

I have a level road before me tomorrow; my direction is due north, and I hope to make Gannat, 20 miles from here. I want to reach Moulins by Thursday any way; after that is passed, I shall begin to consider myself in the architectural center of France, with Nevers, Bourges, Orleans, Blois, and Tours before me and the chateaux of the Loire at my side. . . .

[letter recommenced on Apr. 3 in Moulins]

I reached Gannat about 4 P.M. pretty well tired out and only just in time to escape a wetting. . . . The rain over, I sallied out and walked slowly about town until "dinner" to keep my limbs from getting stiff and to note what should be sketched in the morning. I purchased a couple of pairs of soft merino socks to use in walking, for my woolen ones fill up my shoes so that it prevents good circulation. You see, I take the same care of myself as I would of a pet dog or a race-horse.

I found an old church in Gannat and much very good old architecture for so small a place, but it was all in scraps—and scattered all over the town. The church is ordinary at first appearance but develops some very instructive features when examined. . . . I did not sketch it, but studied it. . . .

The following day (the 30th of March) I started for St. Pourcain. . . . One time I made a digression from the road to what I supposed was

Dormer in St. Pourcain

Library of Congress

an old chateau among a clump of trees. It looked promising in the distance, but panned out a factory. . . .

I was surprised to find at St. Pourcain quite a large church and very much excellent picturesque domestic architecture. I had not intended to stay there, but as soon as I had gotten into the town, I knew it would pay to stop over a day at least. It is one of those charming medieval towns like Chester, Salisbury, and Ambert that preserve so much of their original character. The picturesque architecture of the dwellings and stores was so much more pleasing than the church that I almost let the latter "go by the board."

I sketched three houses, a dormer, a finial, a high tower, and parts of two more houses in the day-and-a-half I was in St. Pourcain. All the people were very civil, and on the whole it was the most comfortable, easy place to sketch I have been to yet. Some of the houses are very old;

House in St. Pourcain

Sketchbook 1, New-York Historical Society, negative 75224

Dated lintel on a house in St. Pourcain
Sketch in letter

one that I sketched bore the date, almost effaced by time and whitewash, 1205 (A.D) in letters of ancient shape.

St. Pourcain is a place no tourist visits, and here may be seen the peasant Frenchman in his native wilds. It is a jolly old place of much beauty, and I flatter myself in having added another picturesque town to the long list of those already known and visited by architectural students. . . .

I had met but one man who spoke English since I left Lyon, so I seemed once more in civilization when I got your dear letters. Some of them had lain in London, some in Paris; one had followed me all through Italy and half of France. You don't know just the feeling one has when letters come in a foreign land. . . . I am more anxious every day for the time when I shall return home to St. Paul. For although it may be profitable for me to work in Boston or study there, I am fast coming to a firm conclusion that St. Paul is the place for me to live in. . . .

If any one else is coming to Europe, tell them to bring only a hat and a pair of shoes, one suit of clothes, a sketch-book, and a package of lead pencils, and not to leave a cent of money behind them. . . .

My letter from Waterhouse is really quite refreshing. It is a flat refusal. The very flattest kind of flat. Not rude and impolite but very plain. At least he has considered my letter worth answering, which Geo. Godwin (of London) evidently did not. . . .

Moulins is rather a beautiful cathedral, but its beauty is not in the new work. . . . The old part of the cathedral contains what I consider the most beautiful stair way I have ever seen. . . . It is a circular stair way, half hid in the wall, and as it appears and disappears with each successive turn (its balustrade's delicate tracery reflecting lines of light and casting threads of shade), it grows in beauty as it rises until almost lost in the shade and pleasant darkness overhead among the arches. A delicate pier stands all free and alone in front of it and develops into those elegant lines and graceful curves that only Gothic vaulting can produce. . . .

Moulins as a town is a splendid place. Half ancient, half modern, some picturesque, very French, and contains the nicest people I have

Font in Moulins Cathedral

Sketchbook 1, New-York Historical Society, negative 75225

met on the continent. The house I live in is called "le ancien Maison Compagnon" and is about as quaint, as old, and as queer a place as you will see in all of France. It hangs out over the street at every story. It is timbered to last a thousand years longer, it is plastered outside, it is carved, oiled, and time stained. It is colored by nature more than by man, its roof is tiled, its chimneys are high in [the] air, its rooms small with floors of brick, low doors that enforce politeness, steep stairs, and narrow passages. It is ancient. . . .

Mr. Gassmann made friends with me at once on hearing that I was a student of architecture &c. &c. and said he should be happy to call on me. . . . He looked over my sketches and insisted on my going out with him to call on a friend of his and to take the sketches with me. This friend of his is no less a man than the (in France) celebrated artist and etcher Armand Queyroi. I objected to taking the sketches, but as he insisted, I finally consented. Mon. Queyroi is immense. His studio is simply ideal, real old armor, tapestry, paintings, engravings, old chests and cabinets, ancient iron work, and a hundred curious things. I had the rarest treat an American ever had. . . .

M. Queyroi looked over my sketches and praised and condemned them in an honest way that will be a great help to me in seeing my faults. He praised especially my water-color of the Roman Forum and my sketches in St. Pourcain. He looked at the sketches of St. P. many times and has since asked permission, through Mr. Gassmann's interpretation, to copy one that I made there. . . . I was, of course, very much flattered by such attention, for I can well appreciate what it means. . . .

He has given me a card of introduction to Mr. John M. Mitchell, an American artist in Paris, one of the best etchers there. I have heard of him frequently in America.

Mr. Gassmann took me all over Moulins in the afternoon, and although I had thought I had seen all there was to see, yet he showed me things I had not heard of before. He took me to an old chapel whose ceiling was covered with paintings of rare beauty to my un-tutored eye, seeming to equal almost any I had seen in Italy. They were filled with holes, and when it rains the water drips through them. An

La Cour de Madame Gauthier

Sketchbook 1, New-York Historical Society, negative 75226

English nobleman has offered £10 000 for these paintings just as they are, but they belong to the city and can not be sold. . . .

We went to what is called "la Cour de Madame Gauthier" (Goat-yea). It was once part of the chateau (which included all the cathedral, the prison, my lodgings, and half Moulins). It is a beautiful thing, designed in the style that prevailed when Francois I was King. I am getting to like that style immensely, tell Clarence, and when I get into practice he may expect to see the old chateaux and Flamboyant cathedrals instead of English castles and the Romanesque.

I have since sketched "la Cour de Madame Gauthier" and nearly broke my neck in doing it, for the court is only about 25 feet square and the facade I sketched about 60 feet high. The perspective was tremendous.

We went to another court, very much smaller, of similar style and freshly painted with yellow paint, which is very well for posterity (preserving the stone) but unfortunate for the present generation.

I forgot to say that in Madame Gauthier's house was a chimney built in the time of Pierre II in what was then the "chapter house" of the cathedral, now a bed room, which was large enough to put a bed inside (the bed is there now) and allow the curtains to fall straight down, being hung from the mantel-shelf line. It was very well designed and a capital place for a bed. I did not sketch it but have noted it here from memory. . . .

Chimney bed, Madame Gauthier's house
Sketch in letter

[recommenced Apr. 10 in Nevers]

I was in Moulins just a week, and one day of that time was taken to visit Souvigny about 5 miles away. S. is a place I would not have missed. I could have spent a week there, but life is too short (and money also). I will not attempt to speak of Souvigny, for this letter is already too long to suit your patience and two cathedrals are already mentioned in its pages. I have two sketches and a photograph of the cathedral, which will recall to mind its beauties when I return home. . . .

Ruins of the gate at the chateau, Moulins, France

Library of Congress

How strange are the ways of Providence. I was guided through all from the beginning, and out of trouble came pleasure.

My letter, or rather card, to Mr. Mitchell may result in my learning the process and art of etching, which I have long considered the best method of illustrating architecture. . . .

I will leave here day after tomorrow (the 12th of April) for Bourges. My departure may be delayed a day or two, for I have had to send to Paris for a sketch-book, my present one being about finished, and I will wait here until it arrives. I will go by cars to Bourges. From Bourges I make for Orleans by way of Gien. . . . I reach the Loire, my old companion, at Gien and keep by its side until I have passed Tours. . . .

I shall probably go from Tours to Lemans and from there either to Mont St. Michel by way of Leval and Reunes or direct. I have decided to skip St. Malo, Dol, and Dinan, which are so often visited by artists and said to be so picturesque. From Mont St. Michel I want to go to Caen by way of Avranches, Coutances, & Bayeux, and from Caen to Rouen by way of Lisieux. From Rouen I go direct to Paris, where I hope to arrive about the 10th of June, in time to see the last days of the Salon. If possible I hope to visit Chartres from Paris; it is only about 40 miles from there and is the most cele-brated cathedral in France.

I feel that I had ought to visit Normandy if I do not see a thing in England, for by so doing I will see what is considered by all the perfec-tion of Gothic architecture at Caen and Rouen. And then a reason more potent: If I see the Norman styles, I will have seen illustrations of all the principal forms of architecture: English Gothic at Chester and Salisbury; French-decorated Gothic at Notre Dame, Rouen, and Caen; Flamboyant at Moulins, Clermont, and Lyon; Romanesque at Lyon, Clermont, and St. Etienne in Nevers; Byzantine at St. Mark's in Venice; Italian Gothic at Milan, Orvieto, Siena, Florence, and Pisa; Venetian Gothic in Venice; Classic in Rome; Renaissance at Paris; and the varying styles of mixed Classic and Gothic of central France. As yet, Romsey Abbey in England is the only example of original Norman work that I have seen.

Chateau at Nevers

Library of Congress

You can safely count on my being in Paris about the 5th of June. On the way from Paris to England, I will stop at Beauvais, Amiens, and Abbeville so as to get an idea of the Gothic of northern France. The weather for the past week or more has been unfavorable for out door work, and being forced to work indoors or in the sunshine, my eyes are troubling me for the first time since I left Zanesville. I bought a pair of colored glasses today, but they are a little too dark and I shall have to change them. I hope my eyes won't give out, for if they do I might as well throw up the sponge. Writing 50 page letters by candle light has as much to do with it as sketching in a dim cathedral or in glaring sunlight. . . .

Every town now has a chateau and a cathedral. Nevers has a cathedral which is just such a one as I should like to build, in a great measure my ideal. There is another Bourbon chateau there of not a little beauty, a Romanesque church, and some old walls with a moat crossed by little bridges at one side of the city.

To Clarence Johnston, April 2, 1880   **Moulins**

When anyone tells you living is cheap in some foreign place or country, don't you believe it; or at least add 20 per cent to your informant's estimate. You remember our experience in getting lodging in Boston? I do, vividly. Multiply that experience by the difference between your native and a foreign language; add to the product a worn-out body whose travel-racked mind is susceptible to any seductions in the way of repose, no matter what the cost may be, a patience exhausted with ineffectual attempts, oft-repeated, and you have a sum total which, if not actually appalling, is rather startling.

Let me begin: Arrived in Liverpool; anything to get off that d— (doggoned) steamer, you pay a porter 2 shillings to get your trunk and things off and past the custom house. Customs examination done, 1 shilling (25c); take your stuff up to a cab about a half a block away. 3 shillings carries you and stuff to the hotel, and you are lodged cheaply at 5 shillings a day, and boarded too, I may add, and clap-boarded, slabbed, or planked. The next morning you will start for London. Will you, though? Every effort is made to detain you. There is a "gallery" that is found only on certain days; tomorrow is one of those days.

La Porte du Croux, Nevers

Library of Congress

Mr. So and So is to make the greatest speech of the campaign in the public square this afternoon (perhaps it's Gladstone or John Bright; will you miss that?). At the last minute your bill is not ready. "The bill must be prepared. The money can't be received without it," says the landlady. Bill is about three times as high as it should be. Everything charged double, a stack of extras and a dozen things that you haven't had. Of course, there is a row. I'm rather peaceable, but a bill generally has to be made out 3 different times before my taste is suited; sometimes, as at Riom the other day, it comes back larger each time until you are glad to get off, having rescued enough of your baggage and depleted purse to help you on to the next town. (As at Pisa also, in my case.) Everything is charged extra. "Room and board was 5 shillings, was it?" Certainly, but there is the candle, and you burned the best part of the three that were in your candelabra, trying in vain to get light enough to write to your friends at home. . . . Did you ever buy a candle in your life? How do you know that 10¢ would buy a pound of such as you are paying for? Six pence don't seem much, and that is settled. . . . An item of milk is introduced. What the deuce does it mean? You are reminded: When you ordered coffee and the waiter forgot to bring milk with it, you "tipped" his memory. Butter is charged extra with dinner, and possibly in your ignorance you have dined twice in one day. . . . So it goes. . . .

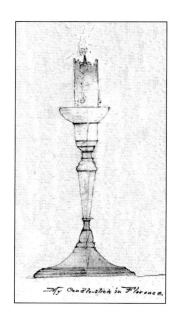

Detail of candlestick, Florence

I am of the firm opinion that it is impossible to live with even the necessaries of common life in London for less than $25.00 a month. . . . I tried numerous places (some 20 in all), many of which were far inferior to the worst living you or I have ever seen, worse than I saw in Wisconsin or on the Hudson River even, and the price simply ruinous: $25.00 per month and upwards, only two meals a day, and fire extra. . . .

A fellow might exist in the summer, but in the damp and fog of winter, every hour would be another word in his death-warrant. Why, Clarence, it is a recorded fact that more people died in London during the week that I was there from the effects of the fog and ordinary disease affected by the fog than during any week before or since the great plague. . . .

In Paris, live in the "Quartier Latin." It is the place for a student and the cheapest part of Paris. At Hotel du Bearn, Rue de Lille, I found a pleasant landlady whose son spoke a little English. He was an artist and a pleasant fellow. I had two rooms at Hotel du Bearn. It seems extravagant to have two rooms, but they were the only apartments unlet in the hotel and must go together. They were only a little more expensive than a single room would be, so I took them. . . . You see, these hotels are different from ours: There is no writing room where a fellow can sit and read, write, or finish sketches. There is no place to dry wet clothes when you come in out of the rain and no place to loiter except in your own room or at the café, which is generally noisy and smoky, and as I have gotten to thoroughly detest tobacco, I don't like cafés. I think if I hated the "old boys" as I hate tobacco, I would be a "solid muldoon."

As to railway traveling in France and Italy, I can speak with some knowledge. The third class cars are, as a general thing, fit only for cattle: dirty, smoky, and vile to the last degree. You may travel 6 hours in one, but I advise you not to attempt a longer stretch at a time. I traveled from Paris to Turin almost without a rest for 36 hours. The result—I was sick in bed five days in Milan. . . .

In going to the large cities like Venice, Florence, & Rome, I bought guide-books. In Rome it is very essential to have a good guide-book, and the information is generally reliable, well written, and valuable, but your own sense of the beautiful will guide you rather than the senseless rhapsodies of the untraveled lunatic who writes the book and praises everything. . . . In Paris, where I expected to spend some weeks, I liked those surprises and unexpected pleasures which are the reward to one who takes his time and loves to poke around in curious corners. . . .

As to buying photographs. . . . In Italy they are the finest I have ever seen, and in all I have spent about $20.00 in this way. . . . If I have to sell my shirt to get home, I'll hang on to those photographs.

To Clarence Johnston, April 12, 1880   **Nevers**

Let me add to my statements in regard to expenses in Europe some few suggestions. 1st, learn French by all means. Bring no baggage with you except a very small satchel and a valise. No trunk. Bring no drawing material. Buy all that in London. . . .

Do not expect to stop in London, for it is the vilest place in the world. . . .

Calculate to be in Italy in the winter, in Paris in the spring (May, June), in London in October.

Do not prepare yourself for the trip by reading up [on] architectural history. Read general history; become familiar with events. Great epochs are the dates in architecture. Styles place themselves when you are familiar with the history of the country in which you may be. . . .

Let your preparation be a thorough mastery of the pencil sketch, figure subjects, arches, and carving. Learn to sketch stained glass in color, if possible. Practice every conceivable perspective, especially the perspective of figures above you and of large tracery windows.

When you buy a sketch-book, let it be at least two feet long and 1'–6" wide, no less if you can help it. . . . I have just sent to Paris for a large sketch-book, having almost completed the one I got in Liverpool. . . .

Save your eyes. You will need all their strength in sketching in the cathedrals, where the light is dim and the object distant. Don't be like me and have to wear a pair of colored glasses when sketching. My eyes have done first rate until a week ago, but are now going out again.

To Elizabeth Gilbert, April 24, 1880   **Hotel d'Angleterre, Blois**

I had a most charming trip from Orleans to Blois. The first day I walked from Orleans to Clerf, about 7 miles. . . . Becoming interested in the great church, I loitered to sketch until the sun went down and the bell in the tower struck seven. It was too late to think of going six miles further, so I put my self under the tender mercies of the landlady of the "Belle Autriche," whose portrait (the autriche, not landlady), painted on an iron sign, swung creaking above the doorway. . . .

Louis XI was buried in the church by his own choice, thinking perhaps that here, as a king, his grave would be honored; elsewhere, where kings were frequent, his bones would receive the disrespect they deserved. . . .

Some of the fellows in Paris told me to allow at least two days for Beaugency. B. is a nice little town but don't pay to stay at long. Hotel St. Etienne and Hotel l'Eau were both too expensive, so I got a room at Hotel Collier. It looked very suspicious and rather like the Snelling House in St. Paul, but on consideration of its being only 5 francs a day, concluded to try my luck there. . . . During the night I heard noises down stairs and once I heard steps coming along the hall-way, apparently stopping at my door to listen. I was a trifle nervous but had a good grip on my pistol. The steps passed on and quietness reigned again. I slept uneasily the rest of the night and was glad to see the light in the morning. . . .

The landlord insisted on taking me to visit an ancient Romanesque house that had a great stone chimney of the time of Francis I. He also got the key and took me into the church of St. Etienne, now used as a wood house, one of the oldest churches in France. . . . I got a good start for Chambord at 9 o'clock, and, with a large sheet of sketches made by a busy pencil the afternoon before, I felt I had done my duty by Beaugency.

I reached Mer about 11 o'clock. Mer is a small town mentioned in the guide-book only as a railway station. In passing through the town I stopped to sketch the turret that ran up at one corner of the church tower. It is a very elegant bit of late Gothic design and really quite an accession to my sketch-book. While I was sketching, a procession of the villagers passed by. Several of them broke ranks to come and see what I was up to, and, the line once broken, the whole procession, drum major, buglers, and all, came and gathered around. They soon got sick of it and returned to their places. About a mile from Mer I crossed the Loire again, by a suspension bridge, passed the little town of Muides, and was soon in the village of St. Di. Here was a large old church of no particular interest except that it was about half and half Gothic and classic, probably built about the same time as Chateau Chambord. . . .

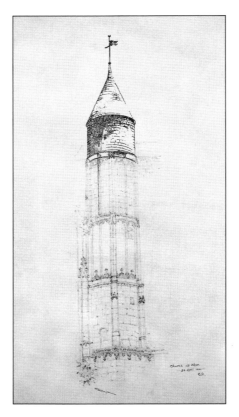

Church tower at Mer
Library of Congress

The chateau is in the midst of a forest that covers quite a large tract of
land and is surrounded by a high rough stone wall with occasional
gates. Passing through one of these gates I was on a wide avenue lead-
ing straight up to the chateau. The road was broad and well kept up,
but the shrubbery and trees on either side were let run wild as nature
put them. They were about such trees and such an undergrowth as we
used to see on the drives from St. Paul to Como [Lake] or White Bear
[Lake]. In fact, the whole general appearance of this country is remarkably similar to many parts of Minnesota; where it lacks [the] natural
beauty of our scenery the deficiency is supplied by a ruined tower, a
village church spire, or an old chateau. . . . At Chambord I went to
the "Grand Hotel St. Michel," which is the only inn at the place. . . .
Before dinner I went out to take a look at the chateau. I walked all
around it, and crossing the lawn where Francois Premiere and his gay
court used to revel and where the courts of Dunois and the nobles of
Blois used to assemble for their hunts, I picked a few more wild flowers
and send them with the violets. Chambord is almost an ideal palace.
It does not remind one of a prison nor of a fortress; it is like nothing
else architecture has ever produced. It is not beautiful as architecture,
but as a well preserved specimen of the style which prevailed when
dwellings were no longer calculated to serve as forts and were

commencing to be considered for civil purposes. Up to the roof it is harmonious, massive, and quiet, rather beautiful with its great round pavilions and continuous lines. Above the cornice it is as disordered as a maniac's brain (rather a good comparison): all towers, dormers, chimneys, and finials. Everything decorated to the last extent, with classic carving and black slate inlaid in the white stone.

Roofs go every way. Chimneys are as high as the towers. Scale is entirely lacking. Proportion was never considered. Perspective effect is out of the question; I found it impossible to tell whether certain features were near or far, whether they were intended for chimneys on my side of the building or for towers rising from the other side. A more confused mass of lines and decorated surfaces I never saw. It is such a place as Hans Christian Andersen would probably have peopled with an ogre, a fair princess, and a youthful knight who rescues her by the wonderful use of charmed rings and incantations. . . . The interior is a labyrinth of rooms and hallways, some of which are in excellent taste and fitted up as they were at first. Must have been splendid in color and rich tapestry. . . .

From the "lantern" there is an excellent view extending to the towers of Blois and far across the forest of Chambord until it is lost on the horizon.

Chateau Chambord was commenced by Francis I on his return from captivity in Spain, and the guide-book says he employed 1,800 men on it constantly until his death. In America 1,800 men would finish it in 18 months or there would be a row with the contractor, sure. . . .

[letter recommenced May 2 in Paris]

I had hardly gotten out of the forest at Chambord when it commenced to rain. Covering my sketch-books with my coat as best I could I ran across the fields to a little old stone church, where I stayed . . . half an hour and again took up the march. I had made about $2^1/2$ miles when another shower came up. I was near a farm house and took refuge therein, despite the growls and barkings of a large dog. I soon got into conversation with the old peasant farmer and found him unusually intelligent. I told him I was an American, and when he heard that he went to the closet and brought out a paper. A newspaper, and an

American one at that. . . . The paper was printed in New Orleans and was three pages of French to one of English. It was a miserable, radical (copperheaded), rebellious thing, filled with scurrilous abuse of every body; I wouldn't have used it for kindling a fire at home, but here in France it was a great treat. I gathered from it that Grant was about to become emperor and that the negroes were to be made nobility—I suppose it is all true.

I translated the English page into bad French for my host and ended by saying the editor was a horse thief and a scoundrel, a deep dyed traitor—all of which was a matter of some surprise to my generous host, who calmly informed me that the editor, Monsieur Gentil, was his brother, of whose literary ability he was not a little proud. . . .
I reached Blois at half past four P.M. 22nd April, just 18 days ahead of the time I had marked on my map, when at Lyon I scheduled my routes and considered Blois one of my main points. . . .

Chateau at Blois
Library of Congress

All these people in the valley of the Loire from Orleans down are a remarkably fine lot of people (for Frenchmen). They are far more intelligent than the people in the mountains of Auvergne and the region around Clermont. They talk better, work harder, and eat less. [They] are larger and finer looking, respectful, and even a trifle dignified. . . .

Blois has been for centuries and centuries the center of momentous events and scenes that made history. It has always been celebrated for the learning of its citizens, their bravery, and their statesmanship as well as their underhanded craftiness and fanaticism.

The Chateau of Blois is one of the finest in France and was for ages the residence of the Kings. . . . The streets that run up the hillside are often streets of stairs, whose winds and turns open picturesque views and sights of quaint, ancient houses as one follows up the slope; turning occasionally one gets charming views of the peaceful scenery of the Loire and the flat prairie land beyond covered with vineyards and here and there spotted with a straggling village or a small stone spire. . . .

The chateau is on the highest ground around and in old times was perhaps a very well fortified place. Three sides of it are inaccessible because of a steep precipice some 35 or 40 feet high. . . . Passing under a couple of groined arches the court yard is reached. It has work of many periods on its different sides, but the most elegant thing of all is the grand exterior stairway celebrated throughout the world as one of the great triumphs of the renaissance. . . . As a lover of architecture, leaving prejudice beyond, forgetting style, I am forced to class this stairway as among the most excellent bits of design I have seen. . . . I had made up my mind to be disappointed. I did not expect such beauty. . . .

In Virune, a suburb of Blois on the opposite side of the river, is a church of very "late decorated" style of considerable interest. I sketched a turret which runs up near the rear of the building, and as soon as I can put [it] in ink I shall offer it to the "American Architect." It is one of the richest and most elaborate bits of Gothic on the Loire. . . .

When I left Blois, Mr. Reid the Scotchman offered to accompany me as far as Chateau Chaumont, the first day's walk. I was glad of

Tour d'Argent, Blois

Library of Congress

the company, and we two young fellows had a pleasant day telling over our hunting experiences, he in the mountains of Scotland, I on the prairies of Minnesota, as we trudged along. When we reached Chaumont I went to the only hotel to leave my "stuff" before we went up to the castle. We learned at the hotel that the Duc de Broglie was at the chateau with his suite, and in consequence the whole town was filled with the attachés of the party. I could have a room, but I would have to sleep with a Frenchman, I was told. This I would not do, for ten chances out of twelve it would be a groom or footman I would have for a bed fellow. I am rather democratic but I could not stand that, so I determined unless the hospitality of the chateau was thrown open to me, I would push on to Amboise. . . .

I saw the Prince and spoke with him and then did a lot of sketching. Before I left, the warder brought me a bottle of wine and some delicate cakes, saying at the time that the chateau was filled with people or a room would have been placed at my disposal. The wine was delicious and supplied the needed energy for a twelve mile walk after five o'clock in the afternoon. Leaving Chaumont I hurried on toward Amboise, a storm being imminent. . . .

The exterior of the [Chaumont] Castle is quite ideal, having great machicolated towers, lancet windows, battlements, and a drawbridge which is let down by chains in the real old style. A deep fosse probably surrounded the rear portion of the castle and parts of it now remain. The castle stands on the edge of a cliff overlooking the Loire for miles, while the little old town with its red roofs, tall gables, and funny chimneys nestles close under it, down by the river side. . . .

[In] Amboise it was not an uncommon sight to see the sign "cave to let." Much has been written on these cave dwellings by the Loire, and Mr. Ware made much of them in his lectures, but I did not think they deserved the attention they have received.

To one who has seen the sewers and beer cellars which are dug in the sand rock at St. Paul by the river side, they possess little curiosity. . . .

Amboise is one of the historic towns of France, and like all historic places in Europe it is also picturesque. Amboise may be ranked as

Details of château at Chaumont

one of the most interesting towns from Orleans to Tours, second to none save Blois. . . .

The great wall of the castle, ninety feet from base to coping, rose up just back of my window, while a little further along was a great round tower almost 100 feet high, twice battlemented and machicolated, loop-holed and turreted in the truly picturesque style.

There is a chapel on the southern edge of the cliff, which is a most remarkable specimen of decorated Gothic. It is very small but perfectly encrusted with detail of great elaboration and refinement, the carving being equalled by none I have seen before for conscientious and accurate work. . . .

To Clarence Johnston, April 28, 1880   **Tours**

Record my hearty congratulations, and accept at once the offer Mr. Ware makes you. You are honored, old fellow, in a way that you well deserve. . . . Surely success is now immediately before you. . . .

Herter's is exactly the place for you, where you will be the companion of Bacon, Riley, Atwood, and Walker. You'll join me in Europe next spring surely now. . . .

I have strong hopes for an opening in a first-class London office in Lincoln's Inn Fields very soon; until the matter fully develops, I shall say no more about it. . . .

If you communicate with any of the people in Boston, send my warm regards to Mr. Letang, to whom I expect to write in a week or so.

My eyes are so bad that I can not write at night.

To Elizabeth Gilbert, April 30, 1880   **Postcard from Tours**

I have decided to leave for Paris at once. . . . My movements have been hasty and uncertain for the past two or three days. . . . Weather is villainous.

Notre Dame, Rouen

Library of Congress

Paris and Beyond

To Elizabeth Gilbert, May 9, 1880   **"Latin Quarter," Paris**

Life in the Latin Quarter is becoming more pleasant every day.
Constantly associated with artists and art students, I can not but
imbibe a morsel of their enthusiastic love for their work. So my
circle of acquaintances grows, and I commence to feel that I really
am one of the students of the Latin Quarter and not an outsider. I
am thrown in their society and made to feel so thoroughly at home
around them that I almost feel like giving up my English trip to stay
with them. . . .

Frequently I find myself at their same table, criticizing and discussing,
telling anecdotes of my tour through France and Italy, and listening to
similar stories, with Norton on my right hand, Foster on my left hand,
Bolton Jones not far off, Vanderhoof across the way, and a host of
others not far behind them. Genial, jolly, yet earnest Norton, the
best American marine painter of the day, whose criticisms are shrewd,
deep, and sometimes bitterly sarcastic, yet never really ill natured.
Foster, a lover of the rural scenery and picturesque Gothic of France,
always careful of his words, never violent in criticism, reserved, calm,
with an occasional flash of enthusiasm making him a charming
fellow. . . . Bolton Jones, sparkling with the humor of queer suns in the
farther countries of the north, a bright eye and a well kept business-
like air give him little the appearance of one who paints the rich,
luxuriant landscapes of Algiers and all North Africa. . . .

Foster has been here for the last four hours, looking over my sketches
and photographs. . . . I must record for you what [he] has just said of
my last sketch. Said he: "That is the finest sketch of Saint Germain
des Près I have ever seen." Of the same sketch Longfellow has said,
"It can't be beat," and Chamberlain, "The form and perspective is
perfect." . . . I am more proud to receive such praise, although mingled
with criticism as it sometimes is, than any amount of "mentions" at
the Ins. in Boston, however much I like the Ins.

St. Germain des Près
Library of Congress

The work I have been doing for the past two months, and which, although I thought it was good, was so far below what I would like to do, I find receives praise and criticism from all the fellows, and every day I have a new visitor to see what I have been doing. . . .

Every impulse is, naturally, quickened to excel, and [I] hold my own among the students here. My mistakes, which are so many I find, are often corrected by a kind word from the elder ones (for I find myself one of the younger ones among fellows, few of whom are under twenty-five and some of whom are little under forty, yet all are "students" and proud to call themselves so over here). How can I help improving when such a crowd help me on? I find myself less giving to the admiration of the "bold," the brilliant, and "striking" work and more inclined to study the modest, simple styles. I find I take more care with what I do, I more easily detect mistakes, I better appreciate sculpture and painting than before, not less appreciating architecture. I am afraid I shall be spoiled for the drudgery of office work and the misery of detailing and preparing "working drawings" unless I get back again right soon into an office. . . .

I have written a lot of Egotism now, and every thing has been about myself. But I know you will not misunderstand me, for I write to you as to no one else, who will pardon all my little self-glorifications and join with me in the pleasure of all these little triumphs. . . . The time will come soon enough when I will work and lack praise, when I will do my best for those [who] will not appreciate my work, when the cares and hard work of business will destroy these dreams of idealism and this association with artists. Why may I not now enjoy what is probably the golden period of my life? . . .

Wednesday next I am going down to Chartres if the weather is good and will probably stay there the rest of the week. I go prepared to work and expect to bring a dozen sketches back, which I wish to be my "chef d'oeuvres" of France. However, I may be disappointed; about such things one can never tell before hand. When I return from Chartres, my whole time will be employed in finishing up sketches and visiting galleries of paintings. I also must go out to Versailles, to St. Cloud (pronounced by all "San Clu"), and to St. Denis.

"In le soir," Chartres

Library of Congress

In London I shall make a thorough canvas of all the offices and do my best to find work, for if there is any hope of Clarence being over here next fall, I want to prepare for a run through Spain, or, if he comes in the spring, to take the summer in Holland, Belgium, Germany, and north France. If he does not come, and I am not receiving pay sufficient to lay by a few pence a month, I had just as lief come home to America. Should I fail to get work in London, I will try in Manchester and Southampton,

Notre Dame, Chartres

Library of Congress

and, should I work my way so far north, at Edinburgh. With Englishmen my nationality is against me, for they can't conceive of architecture existing in America. My hopes are strong for success in London, however.

To Elizabeth Gilbert, May 23, 1880   **"Latin Quarter," Paris**

If I go to Germany, I will almost certainly miss Rouen, Amiens, and Beauvais, though I might take in Rheims on the way back. . . .

I would go without hesitation if I thought you could afford it, but it does seem really heartless of me to be over here spending your money and running around the world as though I were a millionaire. I really

Porte Guillaume, Chartres
Library of Congress

St. Denis near Paris

Library of Congress

am getting to feel ashamed of myself and almost like a thief every time
I draw on my letter of credit. It does seem too bad that you should be
wasting any more money on me.

When I got your letter, I had just made up my mind to stay in Paris
for a month longer and then start for Rouen and England: once more
in London, to gather all my forces and, with my work under my arm,
to try my future with the architect; should I fail, to send my finished
sketches to the "American Architect" and write applications to
different members of the profession in New York and Boston. . . .

I almost hate to start off again alone in a strange country, not
knowing a single word of the language. And another thing: I have
been so long out of an office that I find I am losing much that I
gained while with Clarence in Radcliff's office, and that I ought to
get to work again in earnest soon if I wish to be worth anything
to anybody or to myself. . . .

I have just obtained permission of the Minister des Beaux Arts to copy
some of Viollet-le-Duc's drawings, which are at present being exhibited
at the "Hotel Cluny," and as this may be considered a rare opportunity
and a great favor, I shall not neglect it. Viollet-le-Duc died last spring,
and in some manner unknown to me, his work seems to have become
the property of the state. He was probably the most celebrated architect France has ever produced, an archaeologist second to none, an
authority of the highest order in medieval work and history; his
restorations of ancient buildings made him above all others, except,
perhaps, Sir George Gilbert Scott or Norman Shaw.

To Elizabeth Gilbert, June 22, 1880   **Postcard from Paris**
I leave Paris for Beauvais, en route to England, this afternoon. . . .
Have just met two Boston fellows en route to Greece and all Europe.
Awfully sorry to leave Paris.

To Elizabeth Gilbert, June 24, 1880   **Postcard from Beauvais**
Have been at Beauvais two days; it is a most lovely place. Leave for
Amiens in 10 minutes. Will be there a day or two. Then on to Rouen.

Medieval buildings on Rue de l'Ecu, Beauvais

American Architect and Building News

Beauvais is full of old architecture and has an unfinished cathedral, a palace, some old churches, and some of the queerest old houses. One of the latter is almost entirely built of tile.

To Elizabeth Gilbert, June 26, 1880   **Postcard from Rouen**

Am having a lovely trip; these towns exceed all my expectations. Especially may I say it of Beauvais. Notwithstanding rain I have done an enormous lot of sketching since I left Paris, and, I may say, have done it better than usual. . . . Have just been taking a stroll and am convinced that this is the most wonderful town in all Europe for architecture.

To Elizabeth Gilbert, July 2, 1880   **Postcard from Rouen**

I am about to leave Rouen for Lisieux, via Serguigny. I found Rouen so interesting that I gave it a day more than I had planned.

To Elizabeth Gilbert, July 2, 1880   **Postcard from Lisieux**

I arrived here two hours ago and am now waiting for Hamlin. We will probably go on to Caen tomorrow about noon. Have just been taking a stroll about the city; it is one of the most charming old places I have yet been to. A real old Normandy town.

To Elizabeth Gilbert
July 4, 1880
Postcard from Caen
This morning we went to the English Church [in Caen] and then took a walk out to the abbey founded by William the Conqu'rs queen, Matilda, and to the castle.

To Elizabeth Gilbert
July 5, 1880
Postcard from Honfleur
Will go to Havre by steamer and transfer there for Southampton. Am quite well and rejoicing in the view of soon being where English is the common language.

Street scene, Amiens
Library of Congress

Tower in Caen

Journey's End

To Elizabeth Gilbert, July 18, 1880   **Bloomsbury, London**

Since reaching London I have been almost constantly busy in hunting
work. I have been most unfortunate so far, and although everybody
treats me politely and many even put themselves to trouble in my
interest, they offer but little hope for me.

It is very discouraging indeed: No one seems to want me, yet all praise
my work. They all say a good word first and then end by telling me
there is no use to try to find employment here in London, everything
is full, and that where English draughtsmen are out of work, it is
unreasonable for an American and a stranger to expect it.

I have determined to advertise in the "British Architect," but that is
expensive and offers but small hope. Still, I will try it.

I have come to the conclusion that now is the time for me to accept
your offer, that whenever I wanted to return you would furnish the
money for me to come on. I am ready to leave for America the
moment I have money enough to pay my passage, and the sooner
the money comes the better.

You have no idea how I feel to have to write this; to have to say
that nobody over here wants my work at any price, that I have
tried my best to find work and can not even find enough to pay
for my board.

Can you send me the money to pay my return to New York or
Boston? I am sure I won't have to pass both of these cities without
getting a position.

Until the money reaches me, I am going to continue to look for
employment; but should I be unsuccessful, I will be ready to sail
between the 15th and 20th of August. . . .

There seems to be one chance left, however, which offers hope, and it is this: Mr. Pearson, R.A., who is the architect of the new Truro Cathedral about to be built, has written a note to Mr. Cheney (Prof. Hilgard's friend) . . . saying he would be happy to see us Monday morning and inviting me to bring specimens of my work. There is a bare chance that he may want me. I will go to see him in the morning. . . .

While I am waiting for work, Mr. Cheney has offered to get permission for me (from Dean Stanley) to sketch in Westminster Abbey and will gain for me what other facilities he can. He is very kind indeed, and I feel that I owe much to Prof. Hilgard for it all.

To drop this subject a while, I have seen Queen Victoria, the Princess Beatrice, Prince and Princess of Wales, Prince Christian and the Princess, the two sons of the Prince of Wales, the Duke of Edinburgh and the Duchess, the Duke of Cambridge, Sir Garnet Wolsely, the Duke of Connaught, and many of the notable people of the Court this last week. They were at the grand review at Windsor Castle. I will write you a full description in my next [letter] if I have nothing more important to write.

Detail of Museum of Natural History, London
Sketchbook 2, Library of Congress

Museum of Natural History, London

Library of Congress

To Clarence Johnston, July 18, 1880 Bloomsbury, London

A day or two ago my friend Alfred Hamlin sailed for New York . . . we were old traveling companions and fellow students.

Chimneys at
Lowther Lodge, London
Sketchbook 2, Library of Congress

My dear fellow, I am clean discouraged; there is no use, I can not find work here in London, and I am fast running out of money too. I have tried pretty nearly every where and without success. There is positively nothing for a draughtsman to do unless he is willing to go into an office and work and wait in its most literal sense. I have tried very hard indeed and well nigh exhausted the patience of my friends, yet chances seem no better.

I will soon have to sail for New York; that is, if I can get money enough to pay my passage. And unless something happens before very long, you may expect to see me in less than six weeks.

Is there the least chance of finding work in New York or Boston? Is there anything doing at all? Can you not keep your eyes open and bespeak a place for me should you hear of one? . . .

I never did feel quite so anxious to find work and never have seen the time when work was quite so necessary. Do your best for me, old fellow. . . .

Dormer at University of Cambridge
Sketchbook 2, Library of Congress

I write you these few lines merely as a note to let you know how I am and to stir you up to writing me, and not as a letter; under the circumstances, you can hardly expect a letter. I feel too blue to write anything interesting and I forgo the attempt.

To Elizabeth Gilbert, Aug. 11, 1880   **Ely**

At the advice of Mr. Stanton, I have come up to Ely for a day or two's sketching. My time in London was being wasted entirely while waiting there. Yesterday I stopped over at Cambridge to see the university buildings. I left there this morning and have just arrived. Will go to Peterborough day after tomorrow and then to London again.

Plaster column and capital in Crystal Palace, Lydenham
Sketchbook 2, Library of Congress

The fountains at Versailles; photograph purchased by Gilbert in Paris

Avery Architectural and Fine Arts Library, Columbia University

Bibliographical Note

Cass Gilbert's visual record of his first trip abroad is dispersed among a variety of institutions. The Library of Congress holds the lion's share of Gilbert's dated drawings of his first European trip, comprising twenty-two watercolor sketches, eleven pen-and-ink drawings (some with china white), twenty-one detached graphite drawings, and a bound sketchbook with eighty-three graphite drawings, two of the latter with watercolor tipped in. About twenty drawings in the sketchbook are of subjects depicted after Gilbert's return to the United States. In addition to these, four or five undated watercolor sketches are likely to have been executed during the first trip because of locale, subject matter, and treatment.

At the time Gilbert's heirs bequested this trove of his early work to the Library of Congress, two parts of the stack of 1880 European drawings became detached from the rest. Nine of the watercolors were donated to the National Museum of American Art at the Smithsonian Institution, and a sketchbook consisting of sixty-eight graphite drawings, two with watercolor added, went to the New-York Historical Society. This sketchbook is of particular interest as the first that Gilbert filled in his 1880 European tour. It carried him as far as Orleans, nearly at the end of his walk along the Loire. The sketchbook at the Library of Congress takes up his trip from there.

A good number of drawings to which Gilbert referred in his letters, particularly watercolor sketches, have not resurfaced; quite likely some are lost altogether. Gilbert himself was undoubtedly responsible for some of the losses, as it was common practice for architectural students to exchange drawings or make formal presentations of drawings to senior architects in hopes of winning professional favor. As his letters attest, some of his drawings passed out of his hands within days or weeks of their creation, in reciprocal acts of generosity toward established artists who had treated him with special kindness.

Gilbert also collected photographs assiduously in London, Paris, and northern Italy, regarding this as an important supplement to what he was able to record himself. Inclement weather and scheduling pressure kept him from making sketches of everything he saw, and many buildings from which he particularly wanted to learn went unseen altogether. In addition, he was struck by the cheapness and the quality of

Detail of Haddon Hall; photograph purchased by Gilbert in London
Avery Architectural and Fine Arts Library, Columbia University

photographs available throughout Europe, particularly in Italy. This important residue of his early travels is, unfortunately, past retrieval, beyond a few prints that can only be speculatively dated to the nineteenth century. The Avery Architectural and Fine Arts Library at Columbia University has five scrapbooks of European photographs assembled by Gilbert's son, Cass Gilbert Jr. References in letters to Gilbert Sr.'s photograph purchases and internal evidence such as styles of clothing suggest the possibility—and it is only a possibility—that a handful of these, such as views of Venetian palazzi, the fountains of Versailles, and ornamental detail at Haddon Hall in England, might date to his first venture abroad.

The literary record of Gilbert's first European trip is considerably easier to pursue. Two major caches survive. His letters to his mother reside in the Manuscripts Division of the Library of Congress; those to his closest friend are in the Clarence H. Johnston Collection at the Minnesota Historical Society. Every indication is that these were his only major correspondents. His letters home occasionally refer to a scattering of other correspondents among his relatives, friends, and professional colleagues. These have not been searched for; few if any are likely to have found their way into public collections.

Church between Amiens and Rouen

Sketchbook 2, Library of Congress